MW00489601

The Persecution of the Jews in the Netherlands, 1940-1945

New Perspectives

Peter Romijn
Bart van der Boom
Pim Griffioen
Ron Zeller
Marieke Meeuwenoord
Johannes Houwink ten Cate

With an introduction by
Wichert ten Have

VOSSIUSPERS UvA

Vossiuspers UvA is an imprint of Amsterdam University Press
This edition is established under the auspices of the University of Amsterdam.

NIOD Institute for War, Holocaust and Genocide Studies 2012

This publication is made possible by a grant from the Ministry of Health, Welfare and Sport.

Ministry of Health, Welfare and Sport

Photos: NIOD/ Beeldbankwo2, Verzetsmuseum Amsterdam
Cover photo: Razzia Amsterdam-East 20 June 1943 (secretly taken photograph)
Cover design: Geert de Koning, Ten Post
Lay-out: Adriaan de Jonge, Amsterdam

ISBN   978 90 5629 723 7
e-ISBN   978 90 4851 861 6 (pdf)
e-ISBN   978 90 4851 862 3 (ePub)
NUR   688 / 716

Table of Contents

Introduction
by Wichert ten Have

The publication before you is a compilation of articles resulting from recent research on the persecution of the Jews in the Netherlands during
the Second World War. They are based on the presentations given at a
workshop on that topic on 28 November 2011, at the Peace Palace in
The Hague, as part of the conference The Holocaust and Other Genocides. This conference was organised to coincide with the annual meeting of the Task Force for International Cooperation on Holocaust Education, Remembrance and Research. The Netherlands hosted the meeting in its capacity as chair of the Task Force in 2011. This publication has
been made possible thanks to financial support from the Netherlands
Ministry of Health, Welfare and Sport.

The purpose of this volume is to provide international scholars and
other interested readers with an impression of recent developments in
the historiography concerning the persecution of the Jews in the
Netherlands during the German occupation of 1940-1945.

Since the ground-breaking work carried out by Jacques Presser and
Loe de Jong, research into this subject has taken on new dimensions.
Successive generations have asked different questions from different
perspectives.

To a certain extent, the work being done in the Netherlands has re-
flected the international historiography in that it addresses the political
and public responses to National Socialism and occupation, the nature
of the persecution and the regime in the concentration camps. The perspectives of the general population, of the victims and of the perpetrators are all examined, but above all those of bystanders. In this selection

of the most recent research, there is a particular emphasis on the nature of the persecution and the general public's reaction to it.

In his article, Peter Romijn looks at public administration in the Netherlands under German occupation. The role of the civil authorities during this period has long been controversial in the Netherlands. On the one hand there is the image of an administration trying, for better or for worse, to do the best for its people under difficult circumstances. On the other, that same administration was forced to obey German orders and so to collaborate with the policies they enforced. In many cases, that meant participating more or less explicitly in measures directed against the Jews. Long after 1945, the term 'wartime mayor' remained synonymous in common parlance with someone who had set aside his principles in order to keep his job. Romijn's contribution summarises and analyses attitudes within Dutch local government, in particular.

Bart van der Boom presents the results of his research into what the general public knew and thought about the persecution of the Jews. To what extent were ordinary Dutch people aware of the fate awaiting them after their deportation to Eastern Europe? Van der Boom's hypothesis is that that knowledge is highly relevant to our understanding of public reactions to these events, which in turn may offer a pointer to people's readiness to help their Jewish compatriots. His study is based upon his own analysis of hundreds of wartime diaries. As well as describing the methodology of such an exercise at length, he also reveals many fascinating insights into public opinion at the time. This has led him to adopt a clear standpoint in the academic debate surrounding the attitudes of the general population during the Occupation.

Pim Griffioen and Ron Zeller have conducted a comprehensive comparative study of the persecution of the Jews in Belgium, France and the Netherlands. One of their motives for this was the knowledge that a very high proportion of Dutch Jews were murdered during the war: 75 per cent, compared with 40 per cent in Belgium and 25 per cent in France. The key question, of course, is what the reasons are for these differences. Why is the percentage of Dutch Holocaust victims so high? In their search for an answer, Griffioen and Zeller have looked at the nature of the occupation regimes in the three countries and at conditions there during various phases of the war. They have also compared political developments and how the persecution itself unfolded. Their extensive research has resulted in a clear conclusion about what factors played a part in the national differences. And they pay particular attention to local circumstances and their impact upon the politics of persecution.

Prior to their final deportation to the east, many Jews underwent a period of imprisonment at a prison camp or transit camp in the Netherlands. Marieke Meeuwenoord has investigated the situation at one of them: Vught. This also held other internees, but included a separate Jewish subcamp. Drawing upon German research into the conditions at such camps, Meeuwenoord focuses particularly upon the power structure. Her central question concerns the objectives of the occupation regime with regard to Vught, and how these influenced the behaviour of the camp commander. In the past, memoirs and research alike have always focused on the conduct of the guards, characterising it as brutal. Meeuwenoord, however, looks at the interaction between guards and prisoners, and shows that there was more to the regime than terror alone. Her sources include personal documents and inmate records.

One important aspect of the post-war legacy of the Holocaust is the indictment and punishment of the perpetrators. Johannes Houwink ten Cate has analysed prosecutions for war crimes in Germany, and in his article highlights the distinction between those who gave the orders and those who carried them out. At the heart of this contribution are the trial and conviction of Ivan (John) Demjanjuk in Munich in 2011. Originally a Red Army soldier from the Ukraine, he was trained by the Germans as a so-called 'Trawniki man' – a camp guard – after they had taken him prisoner. Having already been convicted once in Israel, but then acquitted on appeal, Demjanjuk found himself facing new charges lodged by German prosecutors. These claimed that he was an accessory to the murders at the Sobibor extermination camp, where thousands of Dutch Jews were amongst those killed. Information about them formed an important part of the evidence against him. Aged over 90, he was convicted of these crimes and sentenced to five years in prison. He has since died. Houwink ten Cate was originally involved in Demjanjuk's Munich trial as an expert witness, and assisted survivors and the descendants of victims during it. In his presentation he analyses the prosecution and the trial process.

The editors hope that this selection of articles will provide the reader with a good impression of recent research concerning the persecution of the Jews in the Netherlands.

Amsterdam, summer 1941. The sign reads: 'V = Victory, because Germany wins for Europe on all fronts'.

The 'Lesser Evil' – the case of the Dutch local authorities and the Holocaust
by Peter Romijn

In August 1941, Johannes Boot, the Dutch mayor of Wisch, a small town close to the German border, wrote in his diary about a Jewish citizen who had tried to commit suicide twice. The poor man, Leo van Hess, could not stand the humiliations and degradation by the German occupiers any longer and felt certain that as a Jew he could not be saved. The mayor wrote: 'What should we do, what can we do? No people are debased more than the Jews. They should get help in order to save them from the terror.'[1] Boot himself knew about Jews in his community who tried to hide, and considered it his duty to support efforts to help them. At the same time, he seriously asked himself the question how long he could remain in office without compromising his integrity as a Dutch official. He discussed the matter with his highest superior, the Permanent Secretary of the ministry of the Interior, Karel J. Frederiks. The ranking official explicitly told him that 'the Jewish issue' should *not* bring him to resign. On the contrary, Dutch mayors, and civil servants in general, were supposed to think of all others who were relying on the trusted Dutch authorities for protection from the repressive measures of the German authorities. In the opinion of Frederiks, accepting discrimination and humiliation of Jewish citizens for the time being was 'the lesser evil' that had to be accepted in order to do a proper job under the German occupation.[2]

The idea of accepting 'the lesser evil' inspired the strategy of the Dutch authorities through the first stages of the German occupation. Until early 1943, the Dutch administration under German supervision to a large degree managed to convince the majority of the Dutch population to refrain from resistance. Only then, a national strike movement provoked by repressive German measures indicated broader dissatisfaction with the attitude of compliance. In the meantime, the 140,000 Dutch Jews had experienced an accumulating process of discrimination, plunder and segregation. In the end more than 100,000 of them would be deported from the Netherlands and killed. In this paper the role of the local authorities during the German occupation will be explored, as well as what the strategy of Dutch administrators, grotesquely labelled as 'the lesser evil', actually achieved.[3]

The leading questions in considering the topic are: 1) in which way was the incorporation of the Dutch state apparatus contributing to the success of the persecution?; 2) which considerations guided the Dutch local authorities through their actual involvement in the persecution?; and 3) how should the implication of the Dutch administration as an indispensable element of the process of persecution be evaluated?

1. German rule and Dutch civil servants

When the German invaders had conquered the Netherlands, Adolf Hitler decided that the Netherlands would be under a civil administration of occupation, under the leadership of his personal representative, the *Reichskommissar* Arthur Seyss-Inquart. The German regime in the Netherlands took over the Dutch state apparatus as an instrument of ruling the country, while Queen Wilhelmina and her Government had established themselves in exile in London. The latter instructed the civil servants to remain in place, and continue their work as long as this could be done in the interest of the Dutch people. Many authors, including myself, and most recently Ron Zeller and Pim Griffioen, have argued that the way in which the German rulers were able to control the Dutch state, and in particular the ministry of the Interior and the Police, has been a crucial element in explaining the comparative success of the persecution and deportation of the Jews in the Netherlands.[4]

By means of the *Reichskommissariat*, Seyss-Inquart exercised a powerful control over all Dutch state authorities. In name his rule was supervisory, but very soon it actually established strong instruments of steering and control. From the government centre at The Hague, the various ministries were under supervision of representatives of the *Reichskommissar*. These representatives in many cases represented the agendas of the different power centres in Berlin, among them Heinrich Himmler's *Reichssicherheitshauptamt*. Thus, Hanns Albin Rauter took the office of Commissioner General for Public Security within the *Reichskommissariat*, whereas he was Higher SS and Police Chief in the occupied Dutch territories, thus representing Himmler's interests in the Netherlands. Rauter very soon began a concerted effort to take control over the Dutch police. Dutch police organization had been rather fragmented, being divided in six different organizations belonging to three different ministries. Rauter made steps to restructure the police, bring them under the ministry of Justice, over which he took control, and Nazify the personnel.[5] Rauter never completely managed to implement the reorganization. However, he did establish lines of control over the Dutch police, from the central level at The Hague, and from his *Aussenstellen* of the SiPo (*Sicherheitspolizei*) and SD (*Sicherheitsdienst*) reaching to the local forces.

The Dutch ministry of the Interior was brought under control of the Commissioner General for Administration and Justice, Friedrich Wimmer. In The Hague, the Germans established their controlling agencies within the different departments of the administration. By occupying offices within the very building of the ministry of the Interior, they were physically present. Moreover, they required that all internal correspondence at a certain level of administrative competence would be bi-lingual, and that the German text would be authoritative. The highest-ranking Dutch civil servant leading the ministry of the Interior was the Permanent Under-Secretary, Karel Frederiks. Frederiks was a career official, not a National Socialist at all, but one of those who was strongly convinced in their mission to keep the administration running. Together with the other Permanent Under-Secretaries, he had agreed to remain in office under the *Reichskommissar*, in order to safeguard public order and provide for a continuity of the administration as a whole. Frederiks' attitude was, and would be during the whole of the occupation, that the continuity of the Dutch administration was the only way to safeguard the interests of the population. Under his functional supervision, Frederiks had eleven provincial Governors and more than 1,000 mayors. His overall policy was to convince them that staying in office as long as possible should be the fundamental principle of the Dutch administration under the occupation. This would even apply in cases when civil rights of the people and Dutch laws, or the principles of international law, would be violated. Resigning was, in his view, the very last resort.[6]

The *Reichskommissariat* controlled Frederiks and his bureaucracy, as well as the provincial governors and the mayors. The Dutch field administration was controlled on a day-to-day basis by representatives of Seyss-Inquart in the provincial capitals and in the three major towns. In the original and rather complicated Dutch system, the responsibility for policing the public order was – to put it in a simplified way – shared between the mayors, under the ministry of the interior, and the five Solicitors General, acting as Directors of Police in the legal subdivisions of the central state. What Rauter did was centralize control over the police, take most of the responsibility away from the mayors, in particular those in the larger towns, and put it in the hands of the ministry of Justice. At the same time, he replaced the Solicitors General with Dutch Nazis and sympathizers. Thus, the Dutch local authorities were put under firm control in general, and under even firmer control with regard to maintenance of the public order. Dutch mayors tried to find ways to deal with the supervision of the provincial representatives of Seyss-Inquart, even if these officials often behaved unpleasantly and harshly. However, they really came to fear the Solicitors General, who did not hesitate to threaten them with arrest by the German *SiPo-SD Aussenstelle*, and internment in a concentration camp.

Thus, the German authorities in the *Reichskommissariat* took control over the Dutch executive, including the Dutch police, in such a way that they could expect it to serve German purposes. Nazification of the police as such was one of the top priorities, formulated with the purpose of safeguarding the 'public order' in the occupied Netherlands. Public order might sound like a neutral matter, but in the context of the National Socialist regime of occupation, it was, of course, connected to the regimes' concepts of how to shape a society in which discontent and resistance were repressed and enemies of the regime, most of all the Jewish section of the population, would be persecuted. This brings us to the question how it was that the Dutch authorities generally complied – and why.

2. Persecution of the Jews and the involvement of the Dutch authorities

An outline of the persecution of the Dutch Jews may be appallingly brief:[7] from October 1940 onwards, the German regime of occupation managed to organize and set in motion a cumulative process of discrimination, spoliation and segregation of the Jewish part of the population. In mid-July 1942, the first deportation train from the transit camp at Westerbork left for Auschwitz, taking away 1,137 people.[8] Thus, within a period of 21 months, systematic persecution was turned into organized mass-killing.

In October 1940 the German authorities in The Hague required of all people working in public offices and services to make a statement about their possible Jewish roots. All but seven in the whole country, and on every level of the civil service, complied and filled in the form. During the next month, 2,090 civil servants who actually had notified the authorities that they had Jewish roots were dismissed. A next step was forced registration, from early 1941 onwards, of all Jewish citizens. This resulted in administrative segregation of the Jews. Within the registry offices in the town halls, as well as in a central office in The Hague, all Jews were registered as such by name and address. At the same time, a mandatory personal identity card was introduced for all citizens, and those for Jewish citizens were branded by a black letter J. More than a year before the yellow Star of David was introduced as a badge, Jews could easily be identified.

What brought the Dutch authorities, and their personnel, to cooperate in the process; which was clearly in violation of the Dutch constitutional order? In general, the fate of the Jewish section of the population simply was not at the top of their list of priorities. Those who defined the policy of the administration, and Frederiks in the first place, reasoned from a point of view of 'responsibility'. They aspired to remain responsible within their own realm and assumed that by means of such an attitude they would serve the interests of the population at large. To this effect they had been instructed in general terms by the pre-war Government anyway. They feared that taking a stand and provoking conflict with the German rulers in an effort to stop the discrimination of the Jews would render this overall strategy impossible. As we have already seen, this was what Frederiks told Boot.

Moreover, when the issue arose, the Dutch administration felt very much up to the assignment of remaining in office and protecting the population at large. Even though in May 1940 the Dutch army had lost the war, the Dutch civil service felt that it had stood the test of the invasion. They had remained in place, taking all required measures to counter the emergency and safeguard the interest of the people. They thought they would be able to acquire the respect of the occupier by means of responsible behaviour and could capitalize on that. Frederiks and his followers therefore developed a strategy of building upon the idea of a 'common interest': safeguarding public order with the purpose to keep social life going as much as possible. They were extremely concerned about mass unemployment and food shortages and for that reason felt urged to comply with German requirements concerning working for the German military.

During the first year of the occupation, the political situation developed in such a way as to reinforce such a judgment. From the late summer of 1940 until the spring of 1941, the whole country saw an unexpected wave of unrest and violence. This was effectuated by the members of the Dutch Nazi movement – the *Nationaal Socialistische Beweging* (NSB). They took to the streets aspiring to gain more influence by intimidating the representatives of the 'old order' and the newly emerging political mass movement 'Nederlandsche Unie'. The Dutch police and their leadership at the time were uncertain and hesitant about how to deal with the Nazi effort to assume power. The Dutch Interior and Justice authorities, who at the time still had a degree of control, tried to find out the exact intentions of the German authorities. Their overall fear was a takeover of positions by the NSB. At all levels of the civil service, Dutch officials considered the German authorities to be much more reliable than the indigenous Nazis, who had a reputation of being fifth columnists and the scum of the earth. Thus, during the early stage of the occupation, the NSB was seen as the main and most dangerous enemy, and not the Germans. Therefore, the Dutch authorities hoped that by maintaining public order they would keep the Germans happy, serve the purposes of keeping the NSB out, and protect the population at large.

This strategy was, obviously, detrimental for the Jewish section of the population. When they were subject to formal discrimination, some protests were heard; for instance in the universities. The most famous case was the speech by Law Professor Rudolf Cleveringa, who publicly condemned the dismissal of his Jewish colleague Meijers. Much more depressingly, the High Court of Justice complied and uttered no recognizable sign of protest when Judge Visser, the President of the court, was dismissed for the same reason. As legal historians Corjo Jansen and Derk Venema state, this attitude represented an utter lack of leadership from the body many were looking at to actually provide guidance.[9] This did not happen, and all involved were left to consider the matters for themselves and draw conclusions. At the same time, this very attitude was in line with the attitude of the civil servants, as promoted by Frederiks. Even though the Permanent Under-Secretaries protested to Wimmer that 'a Jewish problem did not exist in the Netherlands', they complied, supposing it was in the interest of the rest of the population and dismissing protests as 'unwise' and resignations as 'harmful'. Consequently, tolerating the discrimination of the Jews was considered to be the 'lesser evil'.

At the time, the impact of such cautious attitudes on the local authorities and mayors in particular was mixed. The majority followed, even with discomfort – in particular in cases when persecution could be identified with individual people and faces they actually knew. A small minority testified in public that they sympathized with the victims of forced dismissals. Some mayors visited former employees or councillors in their homes, offering practical support. Many others did not make such a stand. They matter-of-factly let things happen, even if they deplored dismissals and other discriminatory measures, which very soon would cut the people involved off from the means to earn a livelihood or be member of society. Their impulse was and remained to think in terms of public order and to discuss matters in legalistic terms.

Thus, in 1941, in administrative circles the argument could indeed be heard that international law permitted the German authorities to take restrictive measures against enemy subjects, in this case Jews, in order to prevent counter-actions from their side; and was not the registration of the population and the introduction of the identity card a measure to safeguard public order in the first place? The reflex of staying in position seemed to be vindicated by the fact that after the February strike of 1941, the mayors of Amsterdam, Haarlem, Hilversum and Zaandam, were removed by Seyss-Inquart, and replaced by protagonists of the New Order.

The strategy of safeguarding the public order proved a failure when the German authorities made clear they wanted to set the agenda themselves. Their reactions to the February 1941 strike made clear that they did not want to wait for the Dutch to be prepared to unconditionally accept the purposes of the National Socialist occupier. On the occasion of Hitler's attack on the Soviet Union in June 1941, Seyss-Inquart gave a programmatic speech in Amsterdam in which he claimed that the war was between National-Socialism and Bolshevism, and that the time to wait and see was over: 'who is not with us, counts as against us!' The summer of 1941 saw a radicalization of the segregation of the Jews, who were forced to stay apart from Dutch society step-by-step, and live in seclusion. At the same time, the German authorities started to Nazify Dutch society, giving political monopoly to the NSB, even though under German control, and replacing more and more civil servants, including mayors, and other ranking officials by indigenous National Socialists. The radicalization showed its ugliest face when in the summer and autumn of 1941 the German police staged a number of roundups in Amsterdam and in towns in the eastern part of the country. They randomly captured 105 Jewish men in the Hengelo-Enschede area, sent them to Mauthausen concentration camp and had them all killed within a few weeks.[10] Subsequent roundups followed in the Gelderland province. This intimidation had a strong impact on the persecuted people, as well as on their environment. Still it did not change Frederiks' concept that the lesser evil had to be accepted, even though evil was more tangible than ever before.

This brings us to the next question: why and how did responsible people relate to the fact that they had become instruments of the occupier's racist and oppressive policies?

3. Strategic considerations

What Frederiks consciously did, and many others in the civil service followed him in that respect, was to rethink responsibility. In the autumn of 1941, Seyss-Inquart instructed his representative in Amsterdam to make the Jewish Council of Amsterdam the only intermediary between the German authorities and the Jewish communities in the Netherlands. Rauter then moved himself in a position of bringing all Jews under the full authority of his SS and Police system. He actually denied the Dutch authorities the right to decide in any Jewish matter, or on matters related to the Jewish population. His purpose was, of course, to segregate the Jews administratively, before they were forced to enter the next stage of their exclusion and disappearance from Dutch society and territory. In March 1942, Frederiks formally protested a German instruction that Jews from all over the nation had to move to the Jewish quarter in Amsterdam. Once again he called for the common interest of 'avoiding friction', but now was seriously rebuffed by Rauter. The German police chief told the Permanent Secretary that he did not intend to treat the Jews as

Dutch anymore. Therefore, the Dutch authorities had to refrain from involvement in Jewish affairs. The top-ranking civil servant, however, made clear that he did not consider stepping down from a position, which had been formally degraded so fundamentally: '*Ich werde mich dem erteilten Befehl beugen müssen*', he wrote to Rauter.[11]

What motivated him once more was the assumption that he could exercise his remaining responsibility as if nothing fundamental had happened. Even though the occupier violated international law, he assumed that his own position was still in accordance with the pre-war Government instructions. He told people like mayor Boot that the Germans wanted to persecute the Jews so badly that he would not be able to stop them. At the same time, he expressed his hope to make a difference in other matters, in particular in avoiding that the Dutch Nazis would take over the Dutch administration. Therefore, he should take care that 'the Jewish issue' would not cause his downfall.[12] Under these circumstances, Frederiks implicitly opted for a new strategy, given the obvious fact that the one of converging interests had failed. His new one was a strategy of shrinking responsibility: accepting violations of his authority in one field might let him keep his responsibility elsewhere. He was, as a matter of fact, aspiring to maintain 'islands of authority' for his own, in the expectation that he would keep sufficient credit with the population as a whole to maintain his legitimacy. But for how long would he be able to keep his feet dry on such islands?

The actual radicalization of the persecution of the Jews offers many examples of this strategy of letting his authority and responsibility shrink. One example may be sufficient here. It follows from the fact that the German persecutors could only be successful in implementing the different stages of persecution because they were able to secure the cooperation of the Dutch administration, including the local administration, and the police. In July 1942, when the German authorities were planning the actual deportations to Poland, they instructed mayors and local police chiefs, by way of the SiPo and SD *Aussenstellen*, to send the local Jews to the transit camp. Many of them were highly uncomfortable about the orders they received and asked the ministry in The Hague for instructions about what to do. Those who objected, or flatly refused to cooperate, however, expressed themselves mainly by objecting to the involvement of the local police forces, quoting the argument that thus they would certainly lose the confidence of their fellow citizens.

Frederiks' strategy led him to protest this specific element of using local police – and he did just the same as far as the arrest of young men who refused to report for obligatory labour in Germany was concerned. From this perspective, he was not completely unhappy that Rauter had taken away the responsibility for steering the police from the local authorities. Still, the mayors had to transfer the German instructions to the local forces, and to the Jewish citizens. Therefore, individual mayors continued to resist, and told Frederiks that they wished to resign. Mayor H.J. Wytema at Beilen, close to Westerbork, told the German police that he – educated as a student of Law – refused to tell his officers to bring the local Jews to Westerbork. He was arrested and dismissed from office. Frederiks explained to other mayors that this was the wrong example: their duty was to remain in office, in order to safeguard the interest of the remaining people and to avoid a political takeover of power at the local level. He tried to influence Rauter first, and when unsuccessful the General Commissioner Schmidt, who was the representative of the NSDAP in the Netherlands, to exonerate the local police from the arresting duties. In the end, Rauter decided to employ primarily German and Nazified Dutch police, not so much as a concession to Frederiks, but as a matter of expediency.[13]

The picture above is of course a brief generalization, and therefore an over-simplification. Of course, the German policy of persecuting the Jews in the Netherlands raised a lot of individual protest, and sometimes from groups of civil servants, and police, such as in Utrecht and Amsterdam. Such protests were repressed rather quickly, however, and illustrate that real collective action from within the public services rarely occurred. Moreover, they exposed the officials with the most moral and critical attitudes, and made them liable for dismissal. Only when the general situation under the occupation developed in such a way that compliance with the occupying authorities lost ground, and discontent started to define behaviour, matters changed. By the end of April 1943, a national strike wave broke out against repressive measures of the German regime, and in many places civil servants joined the movement. Mayors, however, often felt compelled to muffle or stop the strikes, in order to avert harsh German reprisals. Nevertheless, this was a turning point: the authorities no longer told the people to remain quiet and to comply, now society made clear that the strategy of the lesser evil was losing its appeal. For a large part of the Jewish population, however, this was too late.

4. Evaluation

By way of a conclusion, it is important to note that in the first instance, the cooperation of the Dutch local authorities and the police did contribute to the success of the persecution of the Jews. In his research, Peter Tammes has established that in municipalities that were under a National Socialist mayor, the number of Jewish survivors was significantly smaller.[14] Nevertheless, many mayors of the old order, and local police forces, were involved. How should one evaluate the attitude of the ministry of the Interior and the local authorities in this respect? Did the Dutch authorities actually understand what was happening to their Jewish citizens? They may have felt alarmed, but more as individuals and less as officials, and did not manage to provide coherent counter-strategies and actions.

Even though it was difficult to know for certain what the Germans intended to do, nobody could close his or her eyes for the fact that the fundamental rights of Dutch Jews as citizens were violated from the beginning by an occupier who had pledged to let the Dutch legal order remain in place. Many civil servants put their minds at ease by means of formalistic reasoning; but matters as they were, it was still irresponsible to assume that the dismissal of Jews from public office could be founded on international law. The 'policy of the lesser evil' from a political and moral point of view proved to be problematic as soon as evil became more and more tangible, ugly and threatening. Moreover, the question may be legitimately posed as to whether this concept worked and was viable. The 'strategy of the shrinking responsibility', however, helped Frederiks and his subordinates to accept that the Jews were taken fundamentally out of reach of their own authorities. From then on, mayors and their personnel could only clandestinely help Jews who tried to evade German measures and go in hiding. When the formal involvement ended, the stage was changed and informal involvement started; in the words of Boot: the only thing that may save these poor people is going into hiding.

The extent to which they would engage themselves in such life-saving activities was again a matter of individual engagement, not one of collective strategy. The Permanent Under-Secretary Frederiks, in my judgment, has shown a failing in leadership. He failed to understand what the German Nazis were up to, failed to be alarmed by fundamental breaches of the Dutch legal order, failed to imagine strategies not to cope with the persecutions but to counter it and failed to see that 'lesser evil' and 'shrinking responsibility' left the Jews to their persecutors.

Notes

1 Boot, J.J.G., [s.a.] *Burgemeester in bezettingstijd* (Apeldoorn 1968) 84.
2 Boot, *Burgemeester in bezettingstijd,* 119.
3 Romijn, P., *Burgemeesters in oorlogstijd. Besturen onder Duitse bezetting* (Amsterdam 2006).
4 Griffioen, P. and R. Zeller, 'Anti-Jewish Policy and Organization of the Deportations in France and the Netherlands, 1940-1944: a comparative study', in: *Holocaust and Genocide Studies: an international journal* Vol. 20 (2006), nr. 3, 437-473; Romijn, *Burgemeesters in oorlogstijd* and Romijn, P., 'The War, 1940-1945' in: Blom, J.C.H., R.G. Fuks-Mansfeld and I. Schöffer, *The History of the Jews in the Netherlands* (Oxford/Portland, Oregon 2002) 299-335.
5 Fijnaut, C., *De geschiedenis van de Nederlandse politie* (Amsterdam 2007) 105-123.
6 In defense of his policy during the war, he wrote a brochure: Frederiks, K.J.,

Op de bres 1940-1945 (Den Haag 1945). It did not help his defence and he was dismissed from office by the first post-war Dutch Government for failing to take a correct position during the occupation.

7   See for the brief history: Romijn, 'The War', for a monograph: Moore, R.G., *Victims and survivors: the Nazi-persecution of the Jews in the Netherlands, 1940-1945* (London 1997).

8   Hirschfeld, G., 'Niederlande', in: Benz, W. (Ed.), *Dimension des Völkermords. Die Zahl der jüdischen Opfer des Nationalsozialismus* (Munich 1991).

9   Jansen, C., with D. Venema, *De Hoge Raad en de Tweede Wereldoorlog. Recht en rechtsbeoefening in de jaren 1930-1950* (Amsterdam 2011).

10 Schenkel, M.J., *De Twentse paradox. De lotgevallen van de joodse bevolking van Hengelo en Enschede tijdens de Tweede Wereldoorlog* (Zutphen 2003) 65-69.

11 Frederiks in a letter to Seyss-Inquart and Rauter, 16 March 1942, in: NIOD, Collection 20: 'Verwaltung und Justiz, Stab' 283; quoted Romijn *Burgemeesters in oorlogstijd*, 452.

12 Romijn, *Burgemeesters in oorlogstijd*, 454.

13 More examples in Romijn, *Burgemeesters in oorlogstijd*. Chapter 17, dealing with Local administrations and the anti-Jewish policy.

14 Croes, M. and P. Tammes, *'Gif laten wij niet voortbestaan'. Een onderzoek naar de overlevingskansen van joden in de Nederlandse gemeenten 1940-1945* (Amsterdam 2004) 323.

Transport from the Hollandsche Schouwburg to Muiderpoortstation, Amsterdam, 1943.

Ordinary Dutchmen and the Holocaust: a summary of findings
by Bart van der Boom

International Holocaust historiography seems to have reached a consensus on bystanders: while they knew, in essence, what was happening to the Jews, they did not pay much attention, out of a general indifference for others' suffering or a more specific indifference for the suffering of Jews. 'The anti-Jewish measures were accepted, even approved, by the populations and the spiritual and intellectual elites', writes Saul Friedländer: 'not one social group, not one religious community, not one scholarly institution or professional association in Germany and throughout Europe declared its solidarity with the Jews....'[1]

Bystanders thus consciously allowed the Holocaust to happen, by remaining passive or lending a hand. Dan Stone writes of 'the shocking extent of collaboration and anti-Semitic initiative in occupied Europe'; 'enough people – from state officials to peasants – across Europe believed that they would benefit from the murder of the Jews at the very least to remain indifferent and at worst actively to assist or to take part in the murders'.[2] In this view, the Holocaust was not a Nazi project, not even a German project, but a European project – or, if one wants to include American bystanders: a western project. As the boundaries between perpetrators, accomplices and bystanders have blurred, guilt has spread in ever wider circles. Only the victims and those who actively resisted are still considered innocent.

This notion has come to dominate collective memory. The most important lesson of the United States Holocaust Memorial Museum, written by its founding director, is that 'bystanders, by omission, became accomplices of the perpetrators'.[3] And ignorance, he added, was no excuse: 'The victims wanted the world to know. The perpetrators wanted the world not to know. The bystanders wanted the world not to know that they knew.'[4] The museum prominently displays one of the symbols of bystander guilt: the infamous Allied aerial photographs of Auschwitz-Birkenau that were taken in 1944.

Thus the guilty bystander has become a leading character in the story of the Holocaust. His position is defined by three characteristics: his *knowledge* of the Holocaust, which is deemed to have been sufficient; his *sympathy* towards the victims, which is assumed to have been limited if not absent; and his *behaviour*, which is routinely described as passive if not collaborationist.

This sobering assessment has also been applied to the Netherlands. First of all, ordinary Dutchmen are no longer believed to have been ignorant of the Holocaust. They once were: the doyen of Dutch occupation history, Loe de Jong, argued in his 1967 inaugural lecture that contemporaries feared the worst, but knew little, because the information dispersed by the illegal press and British radio was scarce and inconsistent. Too scarce and inconsistent to convince anyone that industrial murder was taking place, because industrial murder, said De Jong, was unimaginable.[5] More than 20 years later, in 1988, in the closing remarks of his monumental history of the years of occupation, he repeated this thesis and stressed that without it, the behaviour of both victims and bystanders could not be properly understood.[6]

By that time De Jong's interpretation, which in 1967 had been well received, was increasingly questioned. New international research, most prominently Walter Laqueur's book *The terrible secret*, claimed that the Allies had known about the Holocaust from at least the end of 1942, when they had in fact issued an official declaration on the 'extermination of the Jewish race'. These terms – destruction, extermination, mass-murder – were used frequently in Allied newspapers and radio reports (and in German propaganda) and found their way into the Dutch illegal press. This seemed to suggest that contemporaries could have known what was happening to the Jews.

Dutch wartime diaries moreover suggested that some did indeed

know. Most famously, Anne Frank wrote that the deported were probably murdered, and that the British radio spoke of gassing.[7] A small study
conducted in the late 1990s found that more diarists used terms like 'extermination', 'mass-murder' and 'destruction'. De Jong, it concluded,
had therefore been wrong; not only could ordinary Dutchmen imagine
the Holocaust, they in fact had known it was taking place. [8] Amateur historian Ies Vuijsje in 2006 argued the same: whoever wanted to know
what happened to the Jews could know. But the bystanders, sensing that
knowledge would demand action, did not want to know and repressed
the undesirable facts. The victims, abandoned by the bystanders, did the
same, out of sheer powerlessness.[9] Vuijsje's study, while criticized by academic historians, was well-received in the public arena.

Which reaction is not surprising, because Vuijsje's interpretation
chimed with the changing view of bystander *sympathy*. The early historiography had attributed the passivity of Dutch gentiles and the collaboration of institutions like the police and railways to feelings of powerlessness, to a law-abiding mentality, a certain distance between gentiles and
Jews and to ignorance of their fate – but not to any agreement between
perpetrators and bystanders. This, however, changed. Beginning in the
1960s, the soothing post-war 'myth of resistance', which stressed the collective suffering of the Dutch people, the passive resistance of the masses and the active resistance of a vanguard, was replaced by a critical, if
not cynical narrative stressing obedience, collaboration and oppor-
tunism. The growing awareness of the Holocaust, fostered by the Eichmann trial and the publication in 1965 of *Ondergang*, Jacques Pressers'
heart-wrenching history of the destruction of Dutch Jewry, fatally un-
dermined the notion of collective national suffering. According to the
new consensus, the occupation exposed the cowardice of the common
man and his indifference towards the Jews.[10]

That seemed to be proven by cold statistics: the percentage of Jewish
victims in the Netherlands is much higher than elsewhere in Western
Europe: almost 75 per cent, as opposed to 45 per cent in Belgium and 25
per cent in France.[11] Apparently, Dutch society had been unusually
obliging. Had not Eichmann remarked that in Holland deportations

went so smoothly it was a pleasure to watch? Notwithstanding the lack of an anti-Semitic political tradition, the Dutch had failed their Jews much more gravely than the anti-Semitic French. Dutch Jews, in spite of assimilation, seemed to have received much less help than Jews in Belgium, the great majority of whom were recent immigrants. When put to the test, it seemed, the much vaunted Dutch tradition of tolerance had proved hollow.

Thus bystander *behaviour* was also reinterpreted. The resistance of the few was no longer regarded as the expression of the sentiments of the masses, but as the exception to the embarrassing rule of obedience. The fact that more than 100,000 Jews had been killed, roughly half of all Dutch casualties of war, came to dominate the memory of the war and was widely regarded as a result of bystander indifference, anti-Semitism and complicity. Where ordinary Dutchmen were once considered victims of German oppression, they had now become guilty bystanders to genocide. As a result, Dutch involvement in the Holocaust has become, in the words of a well-informed outsider, 'a national historical obsession'.[12]

The new interpretation of bystander knowledge, sympathy and behaviour has an appealing coherence: Dutch Jews died in unusual numbers because Dutch gentiles looked away. Considering the number of victims, bystanders must have refused to help the Jews, must therefore have been indifferent to their fate and must also have been unwilling to know anything about it. This, however, is a circular argument: the high percentage of deportees serves as both result and proof of bystander indifference and unwillingness to know.

In reality, the high percentage of victims need not follow from widespread obedience: a systematic comparison of the Netherlands, Belgium and France has shown there are other possible explanations, such as the attitude of the victims or the resolve of the perpetrators.[13] Obedience in its turn does not prove indifference, let alone approval, as it can also be explained from feelings of powerlessness or, indeed, lack of knowledge. Thus bystanders' knowledge and sympathy cannot be safely inferred from their behaviour, but need to be studied separately.

This is what I have aimed to do in my monograph *'Wij weten niets van hun lot'. Gewone Nederlanders en de Holocaust* published in April 2012. Below, I will summarize the major findings.

1. The German case

Such a reconstruction has been attempted before, in Germany. Following the pioneering studies of Ian Kershaw (1982) and David Bankier (1992), in the years 2006-2008 several acclaimed specialists have addressed the question what ordinary Germans knew and thought of the persecution of the Jews under Nazi rule.[14] They have reached a partial consensus.

There is some agreement on ordinary Germans' knowledge of the Holocaust. The mass executions of Jews in the East involved too many perpetrators and onlookers to remain secret. The extermination camps, however, were shrouded in mystery, and occasional rumours regarding mass gassing were generally not believed. Thus it is clear that Germans were neither fully ignorant nor fully informed. They knew that Jewish life was cheap and many died in the East, but they did not know that millions were killed in gas chambers.

But does this mean ordinary Germans knew *enough*? Did they understand that Jews were exterminated *en masse*, by whatever means, and soon very few would remain? This is where opinions differ. Some stress the ignorance of the means and thus the speed of the killing process and conclude that the industrial genocide remained unimaginable and unknown.[15] Others consider the extent of ignorance smaller and less relevant: one did not need to know of Sobibor or Treblinka to understand that genocide was taking place.[16]

This controversy is partly a matter of definition – what do we mean by 'knowing' of 'the Holocaust' (about which more below) – but also of a fundamental disagreement on bystander sympathy: did Germans *care* to know what happened to the Jews? Some, like Kershaw, maintain that ordinary Germans were simply not much interested in the topic and had plenty of other worries on their mind.[17] Others, most notably Otto Dov Kulka, have argued that such an attitude does not so much reflect indifference as tacit agreement.[18] Most recently, Peter Longerich has suggested ordinary Germans consciously looked away from the Holocaust, out of a growing fear of retribution in case the war was lost – a fear which was intentionally stoked by Nazi propaganda. In his view ordinary Germans were neither in agreement nor indifferent, but afraid of the consequences. They may not have cared much about the victims, but they did care about the crime.[19]

This disagreement is difficult to resolve due to the nature of the sources. All lean heavily on *Stimmungsberichte*, contemporary public opinion reports. About 3,700 such reports have survived, of which less than a thousand deal with the period 1939-1945. They discuss a host of issues, including widespread disenchantment with the regime, but are remarkably silent on the persecution of the Jews. This is what led Kershaw to believe that the topic was not discussed much. Longerich disagrees, arguing that the reports do not so much reflect what was talked about as what the regime was interested in. Either way the major source on German popular opinion says little on the Holocaust.[20]

Eric Johnson and Karl-Heinz Reuband have tried to fill the gap by oral history: since the 1990s they have asked large numbers of elderly Germans what they thought and knew about the persecution of the Jews at the time and concluded that between a third and half knew of the Holocaust. These results, however, are of doubtful value, as memories are very likely to have been contaminated by later knowledge and perceptions.[21] Other sources exist, but are scarce: British interrogations of travellers from Germany, judicial proceedings against Germans apprehended for spreading 'atrocity stories', private correspondence and diaries. Letters are more numerous than diaries, but less frank, due to the fear of censorship. Diaries are rare: about a dozen have been used in recent scholarship.

This fundamental lack of sources led Ian Kershaw to conclude, in a recent overview of the field, that interpretations of the German population's stance on the 'Final So-lution' cannot be taken any further. Sometimes historians simply have to accept that they cannot find the hard and fast answers they seek in the inadequate remnants of the past with which they have to deal. New work will, I fear, be susceptible to the likelihood of di-minishing returns.[22]

If Kershaw is right, we cannot know with any precision what ordinary Germans knew and thought of the Holocaust at the time.

2. The Netherlands: sources

We can, however, know what ordinary Dutchmen knew and thought. The reason is that thousands of them kept a diary during the war, of which 2,000-3,000 have been preserved and are available for research. To my knowledge, such a large body of diaries dealing with one and the same short period is unique in the world. As I will argue below, it offers us an unparalleled insight in bystander thoughts regarding the Holo-caust.

Obviously, not all of these diaries are relevant. Many cover only a lim-ited period, usually either the conquest of the country or its liberation. Others cover only one topic, like military operations or scarcity. In both types of diaries the persecution of the Jews is absent, while the topic might have interested the diarist. Needed are diaries that cover at least the period of deportations, preferably the entire occupation, and a wide range of topics. This leaves only a few hundred diaries, of which I have chosen 164 for analysis.

This collection of 164 diaries is in no way representative for the Dutch population at large. To begin with: 53 are written by Jews. These diarists are included because of their overwhelming interest in the topic. The 111 gentile diarists are *not* selected for any specific interest in the persecution of the Jews, but for a wide sphere of interest generally. Un-surprisingly, educated city dwellers are overrepresented, in spite of a conscious effort to include as many workers and farmers as possible. Age and gender are roughly balanced.

The problem that these diarists do not constitute a representative sample of the Dutch population is mitigated by three considerations. First of all, these 164 diaries represent more than 164 individual opinions, as many also report on the thoughts and feelings of others, who need not belong to their own circle. The atheistic small town notary in no way represents the simple god-fearing villagers around him. But in his diary he frequently discusses what they think and talk about. Many Jewish diarists reflect on gentiles' reactions. Secondly, diarists' interpretations can be compared to opinion reports drawn up by diverse authorities in the occupied Netherlands. These are not as numerous or as extensive as the German reports – Dutch police especially reported with visible reluctance – but they do contain observations on popular opinion regarding the persecution of the Jews. Thirdly, and perhaps most importantly, there is a strong convergence of evidence. The thoughts regarding the persecution that the individual diarists express, their estimation of other people's thoughts and the opinion reports correspond to a surprising degree. Dissenting views are very rare. This suggests that there was a dominant popular opinion on the persecution of the Jews; if there had been a significant diverging current of opinion, it should have left more traces.

Thus I believe that a mainstream popular opinion regarding the persecution of the Jews and a widely shared expectation regarding their fate did exist and can be reconstructed. And I believe that what ordinary Dutchmen thought and knew helps explain what they did. These three topics – sympathy, knowledge, behaviour – form the pillars of my book, and will be treated here successively.

3. Sympathy

What did ordinary Dutchmen at the time think of the anti-Semitic policies the occupier introduced? Did they, as dominant collective memory would have it, not care much about it? Were they perhaps in agreement or at least happy to profit from it, as Friedländer suggests? The material leaves room for only one answer: they abhorred it.

That German rule boded ill for Dutch Jews was generally known at the time of the capitulation. Anti-Semitism in the Third Reich had been widely reported – and condemned – in the Dutch press in the 1930s.[23] During and immediately following the German invasion many Jews committed suicide.[24] This was widely known at the time, although the numbers were generally exaggerated. While many diarists understood that Jews despaired of a future under German rule, they also considered the suicides premature. Some hoped the Germans would refrain from anti-Jewish policies, if only because this would estrange them from the population. At first, this hope seemed justified: in his inaugural address the newly appointed *Reichskommissar*, Arthur Seyss-Inquart, said he had not come to impose a foreign ideology on the country. This was generally interpreted as a promise to refrain from persecuting the Jews.

This promise, of course, was soon broken. While the first anti-Jewish measure – the removal of Jews from the ranks of the civil defence organization – seemed innocuous enough, the second caused widespread indignation: in the fall of 1940 Jewish civil servants were first barred from promotion, then suspended and ultimately fired. This did not go unnoticed, as many Jews were employed in education; everywhere schoolchildren and students had to bid farewell to their Jewish teachers. Numerous diarists describe this episode: all express anger and many refer to this as a common reaction. The protestant churches issued a joint public protest against the measure while students in Leiden and Delft went on strike in protest against the dismissal of Jewish professors. 'The decency of the Dutch', a Jewish teacher from The Hague wrote in his diary, 'is one of those things the Germans will never understand.'[25]

The next anti-Jewish move was much more dramatic: as a reprisal for brawls between Jews, Dutch Nazis and German police in Amsterdam, 400 young Jews were rounded up on 22 and 23 February 1941. The roundups caused widespread alarm and indignation and in protest a general strike erupted in and around the city, which was crushed by violence and threats in two days. Although the Dutch press was not allowed to report on it and *Radio Oranje* (the radio station run by the government in exile) kept silent, the news of the strike spread like wildfire. It was received with great satisfaction: this would teach the Germans that Holland would not countenance anti-Semitic violence. A few diarists knew that a strike by gentiles in support of Jews had never happened before. Only the abovementioned Jewish teacher had his doubts: resistance, he feared, could only lead to more Jewish suffering.[26]

In the following months he seemed to be right. The young Jewish men who had been rounded up were sent to Mauthausen. In retaliation for acts of sabotage, another 500 Jews were sent there in the summer and fall of 1941. Soon death notices started to arrive and by early 1942 it was clear that all had died. Mauthausen became the spectre of terror and a powerful deterrent – as was the German intention. There were jokes about everything that had been done to the Jews, one diarist observed, but none about Mauthausen.[27]

Perhaps the clearest illustration of Dutch popular opinion regarding the persecution of the Jews is the reaction to the introduction of the Jewish badge that in late April 1942 all Jews were ordered to wear. Affecting all Jews and Jews only, the star was an unmistakable and highly visible sign of anti-Semitic fervour. The reaction was equally unmistakable: anger and horror. And the anger showed. During the first days of wearing the star, Jews everywhere were treated with demonstrative courtesy: hats were tipped, seats on the bus and train offered, words of encouragement spoken. 22 diarists, Jews and gentiles, from different parts of the country, reported these scenes.[28] The German authorities were sufficiently irritated to instruct the press to warn that demonstrative friendliness towards Jews would be punished severely.

Then, in July 1942, deportations began. While Jews had been sent to labour camps in the Netherlands since the beginning of the year, and *Arbeitseinsatz* of non-Jews had begun in earnest in April, the announcement that all Jews would be sent East came as a shock. Clearly, two years of anti-Semitic measures and violence had not prepared bystanders or victims for what was immediately perceived as a brutal operation.

Where Jews had generally assumed they would outlive the Nazis, some now were no longer sure. Suicide, which after May 1940 had returned to pre-war levels, rose steeply in July 1942; several dozen Jews would take their life each of the following months.

The fear that gripped the Jews did not escape the gentiles. They in no way justified, downplayed or trivialized the violence of the persecutors and the despair of the victims. On the contrary: bystanders rather exaggerated the horror by telling gruesome but largely incorrect stories of violent separation of families, abandoned Jewish children wandering the streets and hunger and torture roaming transit camps Westerbork and Vught. This is remarkable, considering that trivialization or justification of a persecution one feels powerless to prevent is attractive to bystanders: it soothes their conscience and protects their notion of a just universe. Among ordinary Germans these mechanisms were probably quite common. Among ordinary Dutchmen they were very rare.

Many diarists in fact described the deportations as a crime of unimaginable horror and the nadir of the entire war. Even those who had seldom mentioned the persecution of the Jews before, now did. As the deportations continued, scenes of departing Jews became routine, but indignation resurfaced when particularly shocking events took place, such as the roundups in hospitals and old peoples' homes starting in the fall of 1942, the deportation of hundreds of patients from a Jewish psychiatric hospital in January 1943, the forced sterilization of Jews in mixed marriages in May, and the hunt for the last Jews living in Amsterdam that summer. After deportations had ended in September 1943, the topic disappeared from most diaries, only to return when liberation brought stories of untold horror.

All in all, there can be no doubt that the Dutch population rejected the persecution of the Jews. Of the 111 gentile diarists, 92 expressed their indignation in clear terms. Of the 19 that did not, four seem to have agreed with the persecution to some extent (three of them members of the Dutch National Socialist movement), five appear more or less uninterested in the topic, while the remaining ten write very factual and neutral diaries that leave little room for moral indignation. Dozens

of diarists, moreover, described indignation as common. Virtually all diarists, including those with Nazi sympathies, agreed that anti-Jewish
policy was a public relations disaster which further stoked anti-German
sentiment. Many Jewish diarists were impressed by the sympathy they
encountered, while only one or two expressed disappointment about
gentile attitudes.[29]

The authorities themselves noted this too. Public opinion reports describe the widespread unrest, anger and incomprehension regarding
the persecution. The same anger was expressed in the illegal press, in
the protests by the Dutch churches, in the strike of February 1941 and
the demonstration of solidarity following the introduction of the Jewish
badge.

4. Sympathy: the tolerant nation

But what, one may ask, about anti-Semitism? While it had never played
much of a role in Dutch politics, there was a mild but widespread social
and cultural anti-Semitism. The racial and paranoid anti-Semitism
characteristic of National Socialism was largely absent, but the notion
that Jews had their own, not necessarily attractive traits, was common.
Ambivalence between religious and ideological groups, moreover, was
institutionalized in the form of 'pillarization': the existence of parallel
societies in which especially Catholics and orthodox Protestants were
largely shielded from contacts with others – including Jews. Anti-Semitic stereotypes show up in 24 of 111 diaries written by gentiles. Another
36 gentile diarists write too little about Jews to show their convictions.
The remaining 56, however, mention Jews often without showing any
sign of anti-Jewish sentiment.[30]

While the strength of anti-Semitism is difficult to gauge, it certainly
was hardly a topic before the German occupier introduced it. Some diarists believed this introduction in fact diminished indigenous anti-
Semitism. The fact that persecution was a German project predisposed
ordinary Dutchmen to disapprove. Just like ordinary Germans tended

to justify persecution out of a general support for the regime, ordinary Dutchmen tended to reject it out of a general hatred of the regime. The enemy of the enemy became a friend. The strike of February 1941 was both a demonstration of support for the Jews and hatred for the Germans.

Anti-Jewish sentiments probably revived, however, in the second half of the war, when deportations had begun and many thousands of Jews went into hiding. In the course of 1943-1944 stories began to circulate about ungrateful and demanding Jews in hiding, behaving carelessly and even betraying their helpers. That notion was sufficiently common to feature in a range of illegal papers between September 1943 and July 1944. All agreed that reports of misbehaving Jews in hiding led to an increase in anti-Semitism and, occasionally, the refusal to help Jews.

So how do we explain the fact that support for anti-Semitic policies was virtually absent, while anti-Semitism was not? Common enmity towards a hated occupier cannot explain all: in occupied Poland hatred regarding the Germans did not preclude approval for anti-Semitic measures. Crucial to the Dutch attitude was a particularly Dutch phenomenon: the self-image of the tolerant nation.

This self-image had old and deep roots. The merchants that had run the Dutch Republic in the 17th and 18th century had generally preferred social harmony to religious strife and had therefore accommodated pluralism, a pluralism which by the end of the 19th century had solidified into pillarization. In the process the essentially pragmatic attitude of tolerance had been relabelled a patriotic virtue, if not a founding principle of the nation.

The power of this self-image showed when ordinary Dutchmen were confronted with the unusual spectre of brute discrimination of a minority. Disqualification of this practice as contrary to essential Dutch values was virtually automatic. When Dutch churches protested against the discrimination of the Jews for the first time, in the fall of 1940, they reminded *Reichskommissar* Seyss-Inquart of his pledge to respect Dutch culture and tradition – which evidently was not compatible with religious discrimination. Rejection of the persecution of the Jews was thus a patriotic duty.

This sentiment was expressed by many gentile diarists, including those with anti-Semitic inclinations; some first railed against Jews and in the next sentence against their persecution. German informants and Jewish diarists also noted that aversion to anti-Semitic policies trumped aversion to Jews. The attitude of the Dutch, a young Zionist accountant wrote, was summarized by the slogan written on a wall in wartime Amsterdam: 'Let these dirty Krauts keep their dirty hands off our dirty Jews.'[31] The anecdote might in fact be mythical, and after the war certainly suffered from self-congratulatory overuse, but it also describes a crucial fact: anti-Semitism as it existed in the Netherlands during the occupation did not imply support for German anti-Semitic measures.

There can be no doubt that Dutch bystanders were not indifferent to the fate of the victims. Very few people ignored the persecution, virtually nobody supported it. The idea that ordinary Dutchmen somehow did not care about the deportation of the Jews, might in fact even have approved it, is simply false. Which of course begs the question why relatively few of them actively opposed it, many remained obedient and considerable numbers in some way collaborated? That is a complicated issue, but part of the answer is produced by the second question my book aims to answer: what did ordinary Dutchmen think about the fate that awaited the deported Jews? Did they, or did they not know about the Holocaust?

5. Knowledge

The answer depends on what we mean by 'knowing' and by 'the Holocaust'. By knowledge I mean subjective certainty: if contemporaries felt confident about their conception of what awaited the deported Jews, that counts as knowledge, even if the conception was false or based on unreliable information. A myth that is believed functions as knowledge, while accurate information that is mistrusted, does not. By the Holocaust I mean murder upon arrival. That obviously is not an accurate definition of the Holocaust, but it is the fate that awaited the large majority of Jews deported from the Netherlands. And, as I will show, understanding that deportation would lead to an *immediate* death was crucial to an adequate response. Thus the question is: were ordinary Dutchmen at the time convinced that the Jews who were deported were killed upon arrival? The answer is: no, they were not.

To begin with, contemporaries did not at all feel certain about the fate of the Jews. Diarists, both Jews and gentiles, consistently described the destination of the deportation trains as unknown and mysterious. To them, knowing what happened 'over there' was simply not an option.

This was not unusual: ordinary people in occupied Holland generally felt they knew very little about events elsewhere. All media were considered suspect; not only legal newspapers, which were obviously propagandistic, but the illegal press and British radio too. Rumours were rife, exaggerations, wishful thinking and atrocity stories the order of the day. Especially diarists who were used to being well-informed were painfully aware of their ignorance. Many felt they hardly knew what went on in their own city; let alone in carefully guarded camps far away.

At the same time, news coverage of the deportations in retrospect seems revealing. British radio, which was deemed more reliable than the German-controlled media, spoke of mass-murder and gassing of Jews as early as June of 1942, before deportations from the Netherlands had begun. In December 1942 the Allies issued the famous joint declaration on the 'extermination' of the Jews, which especially the BBC extensively covered. Dutch illegal papers consistently called the deportations part of a plan to exterminate and annihilate the Jewish people. And even German propaganda frequently recalled Hitler's 1939 'prophecy' that a world war would spell the 'destruction' of European Jewry.

Understandably, this has led historians to conclude that information on the Holocaust was widely available. A conclusion which at first sight seems to be borne out by the diaries that I have analysed: 40 per cent at some point spoke of the 'mass murder', 'extermination' or 'destruction' of the Jews.[32] However, two out of three diarists who used these terms also imagined the Jews would be put to work and housed in camps. Many Jewish diarists wrote of the extermination awaiting them in

Poland and subsequently wondered whether they would meet friends and family there, considered what clothes or books to take or decided to visit the dentist before they went. Many gentile diarists wrote about mass murder and destruction of the Jews *and* compared them to gentile forced labourers. The illegal press also combined qualifications like extermination with the assumption of forced labour and a prolonged existence in camps. This, to a modern reader, seems inconsistent.

The explanation of this paradox is as simple as it is crucial: terms like 'destruction' and 'extermination' in 1942-1943 did not mean what they do now. These words signified a concrete *intention*, not a concrete *method*. Contemporaries could easily imagine, after witnessing years of anti-Semitic persecution, that the Germans dreamed of a world free of Jews and that the aim of deportation was to get rid of them in some way or another. 'Labour service' was widely regarded as a thin disguise for something much more sinister: mass expulsion to an inhospitable place where families would be separated, the able bodied put to hard labour and the young, the old and the sick left to their own devices. Food, it was assumed, would be scarce, living conditions primitive, medical help rudimentary. In the long run, many would die and the Jewish people in Europe would cease to exist. This is what diarists meant by extermination and destruction. Which should not surprise us, as this is what the *perpetrators* meant by extermination, until they decided upon a much more rapid method in the second half of 1941.

Contemporaries thus understood the genocidal intention of deportation. What they did not understand, was the genocidal practice. They could not imagine the unprecedented speed and efficiency with which the Germans set to realize their aim. Many of our 164 diarists speak of mass murder, of certain death, of torture and cruelty, but not a single one formulates the simple thought that the large majority of deportees were killed upon arrival. The extermination camp was beyond the imagination of ordinary Dutchmen – unsurprisingly, as nothing like it had existed before.

The frame of reference remained the concentration or labour camp: a place where people stayed, where they spent the night, where they lived and worked – until they died. Nobody understood that beyond the concentration camp there was the extermination camp, which actually was not a camp at all, but an installation for killing people, a machine processing live human beings into ashes.

The inconceivability of the extermination camp emerges not only from diaries, but also from the memoirs of Dutch survivors of Auschwitz. Dozens have described how they, after having been separated from children, parents and spouses, entered the camp and asked the inmates where those in the other row had gone. When they were told these had by now been gassed and burned, they regarded this as a cruel initiation joke or a clear sign of insanity. Even after spending weeks or months in a transit camp and days in a cattle car, even after being selected on the ramp, shaved and tattooed, standing within sight and smell of the crematoria, industrial genocide was unbelievable.

That explains why reports of mass gassing of Jews, which circulated from the summer of 1942, had little impact. Several whistle-blowers, like Kurt Gerstein, managed to convince Dutch friends that Jews were gassed in the East. When these friends tried to spread the story, however, they ran into a wall of disbelief. While rumours of gassing did circulate, 80 per cent of the diarists never mention them.[33] Many of those who did write of gassings added a note of scepticism. Others assumed that only those who were too weak to work were gassed, implying that those who could work were not killed.

To sum up: there was no knowledge regarding the fate of the Jews, there were only rumours and suspicions and fears. The dominant expectation was not determined by concrete information, which was scarce, diffuse and inconsistent, but by plausibility and the limits of imagination. It was taken for granted that the Germans were committing a serious and sinister crime; obviously these virulent anti-Semites did not transport an entire people to Poland to treat them well there. One did not need to know anything concrete to assume that the intention was to 'exterminate' the Jews – that is what the Germans themselves boasted. What did not seem plausible, however, what most contemporaries did not even consider, was the reality of industrial genocide.

Thus ordinary Dutchmen understood the end of the Holocaust, but not the means employed. They understood the German problem – a desire to get rid of the Jews – but not the 'solution' they had come up with. They assumed the 'extermination' of the Jews would be realized through forced emigration, hard labour, hunger and disease.

6. Behaviour

Does this matter? Did it make any difference that contemporaries assumed Jews would perish in the long run, but did not know that they were killed upon arrival? Is this not a painfully academic and far-fetched distinction? No, it is not: this distinction is crucial for understanding the way victims, bystanders and even accomplices behaved.

This is most evident in the case of the victims, because they had to act upon their expectations of deportation. While many Jews, especially the urban poor, must have considered themselves entirely powerless, the 53 Jewish diarists I studied did not. Seven of 19 who did not go into hiding explicitly say they could have. This was not unusual; memoirs and interviews easily yield dozens of other examples of Jews who consciously rejected the option of hiding. Moreover, of the 34 Jewish diarists who did go into hiding, at least fourteen did so after prolonged doubts.[34] Apparently, many Jews who did have a choice, found this very difficult. Several describe their considerations at length. These are very revealing.

The argument for hiding was the danger of deportation. While nobody knew what conditions in the East would be like, they were assumed to be harsh, perhaps unbearable, and probably fatal in the long run. Everybody knew 'the East' would be no picnic. That is why victims went to great lengths to gain exemptions, why they committed suicide or why they chose to go into hiding.

The main argument against hiding was the danger of punishment. The Germans warned explicitly that Jews who tried to evade deportation and were caught would be punished severely. Initially this was understood to mean Mauthausen, and thus a quick and certain death. Later it became known that those caught in hiding were sent East marked with an S, for *Strafe*, punishment. While nobody knew what exactly this implied, it was assumed that their treatment would be worse than normal.

Thus Jews faced a choice between what seemed an offensive and a defensive strategy. Going into hiding would either work out much better than deportation, or, if one were caught, considerably worse. This implied that, perhaps, it was wiser to obey, to carefully avoid punishment, and hope to survive until the German defeat, which by the fall of 1942 was assumed to be a matter of months, perhaps weeks.

And this is where the distinction between the reality of death upon arrival and the expectation of death in the long run, becomes crucial. On the assumption that 'extermination' was a time-consuming affair, it was imaginable that obedience was safer than resistance, that deportation offered better chances of survival than hiding. The fact that many Jews vacillated suggests they judged these chances to be roughly equal. In reality, those in hiding were 60 times more likely to survive than those who were deported. If Jews in the Netherlands had known this, they would have behaved differently.

Some bystanders would have behaved differently as well. Diaries show that many did feel for their Jewish fellow citizens. Some were willing to help: 28,000 Jews went into hiding, which must have involved at least as many households, probably many more. Hiding was (wrongly) assumed to be equally perilous for both parties. Thus if Jews could decide that resistance was an unwise choice, gentiles could, too – not out of indifference or anti-Semitism, but out of a faulty appraisal of the risks; out of ignorance of the true nature of deportation.

And this could even apply to accomplices. Policemen and civil servants, or, for that matter, the men and women of the Jewish Council, did consider their involvement in the persecution distasteful and compromising, especially once deportations began. Although very few refused outright, many struggled to morally justify their behaviour. An important part of that justification was the notion of the lesser evil: better to pick Jews up in an orderly fashion than to have them hunted down in the streets; better to send them off well-equipped and well-fed, than unprepared and hungry; better to negotiate than to have total chaos descend on the Jewish community.

Essentially, ordinary Dutchmen remained obedient or cooperative in the face of deportation of the Jews for the same reasons that they did not resist many other measures they despised: out of a paralyzing feeling of powerlessness and a personal fear of punishment, buttressed by a general conviction that resistance would only make matters worse. A conviction which in many cases was understandable; it for instance did and still does seem doubtful whether the benefits of sabotage justified the cost of reprisals. If bystanders had known that in the case of deportation of the Jews, nothing could be worse than obedience, they too would have acted differently.

Not all, obviously, perhaps only a minority. Some felt so little solidarity with Jews they would never have run risks for their sake. Others felt too powerless or vulnerable to ever have undertaken anything illegal. Even if gentiles had known that the Jews were killed upon arrival, their willingness to help would have been limited. But it would have been larger, much larger perhaps. Ignorance of Auschwitz is not a sufficient explanation for the behaviour of bystanders, but it is a necessary explanation.

7. Conclusion

Thus diaries offer a unique insight into the opinions and the knowledge of Dutch bystanders to the Holocaust, which in turn helps explain their behaviour. These insights are at odds with both collective memory and historiography. First, these consider the high percentage of deportees from the Netherlands a sure sign of a hostile or at least indifferent environment. Diaries, however, show widespread sympathy and indignation. Secondly, it is assumed that reports on British radio and in illegal newspapers speaking of the 'extermination' and 'destruction' of the Jews left bystanders sufficiently informed. Diaries, however, show that ordinary Dutchmen did not at all feel certain about the fate of the Jews. To them, 'extermination' was a concrete goal, not a concrete method. Ordinary Dutchmen possessed no knowledge on the fate of the Jews, but only assumptions and fears. These assumptions were grave, namely forced labour under harsh circumstances, but fell short of the reality of industrial genocide, which was unimaginable.

While it is tempting to dismiss the distinction between knowledge of Auschwitz and the suspicion of death from exposure and hunger as irrelevant, it is in fact crucial. Assuming that killing the Jews would take time – which the Germans would not have as they were about to lose the war – it was imaginable that obeying the summons for deportation was less dangerous than disobeying it. Many victims for that reason chose obedience. And if they were unsure of the wisdom of resistance, it should not surprise us that bystanders questioned it too.

The widespread notion that bystanders knew enough about the Holocaust, but did not much care, is untenable. The limited understanding of the Holocaust explains why bystanders who were not indifferent, did not resist either. *Wir haben es nicht gewusst* is, in the Dutch case at least, not a lame excuse, but an indispensable key to a better understanding.

Notes

1 Friedländer, S., *Nazi Germany and the Jews. The years of extermination 1939-1945* (New York 2007) xxi, 190.
2 Stone D., *Histories of the Holocaust* (Oxford 2010) 16-17, 53.
3 Weinberg, J., quoted in: Novick, P., *The Holocaust in American life* (Boston 2000) 245-246.
4 Quoted in: Bloxham, D. & T. Kushner, *The Holocaust. Critical historical approaches* (Manchester 2005) 4.
5 Jong, L. de, *'Een sterfgeval te Auswitz'* (Amsterdam 1967) passim.
6 Jong, L. de, *Het Koninkrijk der Nederlanden in de Tweede Wereldoorlog*, scholarly edition (Den Haag 1969-1991) XII, 1110; Jong, L. de, 'Nederland en de massamoord op de Joden', in: Idem, De Jong, L. de, *The Netherlands and Nazi Germany. The Erasmus lectures 1988* (Cambridge 1990), there 6.
7 Frank, A., *The diary of Anne Frank: the critical edition.* Prepared by the Netherlands State Institute for War Documentation (New York 1989) 273.
8 Voolstra, A. & E. Blankevoort (ed.), *Oorlogsdagboeken over de Jodenvervolging* (Amsterdam 2001) 118.

9 Vuijsje, I., *Tegen beter weten in. Zelfbedrog en ontkenning in de Nederlandse geschiedschrijving over de Jodenvervolging* (Amsterdam 2006) passim.

10 Hondius, D., 'Bitter homecoming: the return and reception of Dutch and stateless Jews in the Netherlands', in: Bankier, D. (ed.), *The Jews are coming back. The return of the Jews to their countries of origin after WW II* (Jerusalem 2005) 108-135, there 127. See also: Idem, *Terugkeer. Antisemitisme in Nederland rond de bevrijding* (Amsterdam 1998) 66; Galen Last, D. van & R. Wolfswinkel, *Anne Frank and after. Dutch Holocaust literature in historical perspective* (Amsterdam 1996) 10, 45; Bovenkerk, F., 'The other side of the Anne Frank story: the Dutch role in the persecution of the Jews in World War Two', *Crime, law and social change 34*, 3 (2000) 237-258, 247-249; Mak, G., *De eeuw van mijn vader* (Amsterdam 2002 [1999]) 274; Moore, B., *Victims and survivors. The nazi persecution of the Jews in the Netherlands 1940-1945* (Londen 1997) 162; Moore, B., *Survivors. Jewish self-help and rescue in Nazi-occupied Western Europe* (Oxford 2010) 250; Klemann, H.A.M., *Nederland 1938-1948. Economie en samenleving in jaren van oorlog en bezetting* (Amsterdam 2002) 22.

11 Griffioen P. & R. Zeller, *Jodenvervolging in Nederland, Frankrijk en België 1940-1945. Overeenkomsten, verschillen, oorzaken* (Amsterdam 2011) 17. For precise numbers see: Ibidem, 900.

12 Lagrou, P., 'Facing the Holocaust in France, Belgium and the Netherlands', in: Diefendorf, J.M. (ed.), *Lessons and legacies. New currents in Holocaust research VI* (Evanston 2004) 475-486, there 480.

13 Griffioen & Zeller, *Jodenvervolging in Nederland, Frankrijk en België*, 654-686.

14 Kershaw, I., *Popular opinion and dissent in the Third Reich: Bavaria 1939-1945* (Oxford 1983); Bankier, D., *The Germans and the Final Solution. Public opinion under Nazism* (Oxford 1996 [1992]); Dörner, B., *Die Deutschen und der Holocaust. Was niemand wissen wollte, aber jeden wissen konnte* (Berlijn 2007); Longerich, P., *'Davon haben wir nichts gewusst!' Die Deutschen und die Judenverfolgung 1933-1945* (München 2006); Bajohr, F. & D. Pohl, *Der Holocaust als offenes geheimnis. Die Deutschen, die NS-Führung und die Alliierten* (München 2006); Kershaw, I., *Hitler, the Germans, and the Final Solution* (London 2008).

15 Longerich, *'Davon haben wir nichts gewusst!'*, 18, 325; Kershaw, *Hitler, the Germans, and the Final Solution*, 8; Herf, J., *The Jewish enemy. Nazi propaganda during World War II and the Holocaust* (London 2006) 276; Bankier, *The Germans and the Final Solution*, 115; Fritzsche, P., *Life and death in the Third Reich* (Cambridge 2008) 264.

16 Dörner, *Die Deutschen und der Holocaust,* 608; Bajohr & Pohl, *Der Holocaust als offenes geheimnis,* 60-61; Johnson, E.A., *Nazi terror. The Gestapo, Jews and ordinary Germans* (Londen 2000) 436-437.

17 Kershaw, *Hitler, the Germans, and the Final Solution,* 7.

18 Dov Kulka, O., 'The German population and the Jews: state of research and new perspectives' in: Bankier, D. (ed.), *Probing the depths of German antisemitism: German society and the persecution of the Jews, 1933-1941* (New York 2000) 271-281, there 277.

19 Longerich, *'Davon haben wir nichts gewusst!',* 194, 321, 323; Dörner, *Die Deutschen und der Holocaust,* 617; Bankier, *The Germans and the Final Solution,* 146.

20 Dov Kulka, O., 'Popular opinion in Nazi Germany as a factor in the policy of the 'solution of the Jewish question': the Nuremberg laws and the *Reichskristallnacht',* in: Corner, P. (ed.), *Popular opinion in totalitarian regimes: fascism, nazism, communism* (Oxford 2009) 81-106, there 81-82, 84; Kershaw, I., 'Consensus, coercion and popular opinion in the Third Reich: some reflections', in: Corner, P. (ed.), *Popular opinion in totalitarian regimes: fascism, nazism, communism* (Oxford 2009) 33-46, there 41; Longerich, *'Davon haben wir nichts gewusst!',* 38-53.

21 Reuband, K.H. & E.A. Johnson, *What we knew. Terror, mass murder and everyday life in Nazi Germany: an oral history* (Londen 2005) 392-397; Bajohr & Pohl, *Der Holocaust als offenes geheimnis,* 64; Dörner, *Die Deutschen und der Holocaust,* 15; Longerich, *'Davon haben wir nichts gewusst!',* 239.

22 Kershaw, *Hitler, the Germans, and the Final Solution,* 11.

23 Vree, F. van, *De Nederlandse pers en Duitsland 1930-1939. Een studie over de vorming van de publieke opinie* (Groningen 1989) 310-317.

24 188, to be precise. Ultee, W. & Ruud Luijkx, 'De schaduw van een hand. Joods-gojse huwelijken en joodse zelfdodingen in Nederland 1936-1943', in: Flap, H. & Wil Arts (eds.), *De organisatie van de bezetting* (Amsterdam 1997) 55-76, there 63.

25 Italie, G., *Het oorlogsdagboek van dr. G. Italie. Den Haag, Barneveld, Westerbork, Theresienstadt, Den Haag, 1940-1945 bezorgd door Wally M. de Lang* (Amsterdam 2009) 103.

26 Italie, *Het oorlogsdagboek van Dr. G. Italie,* 129, 132.

27 Bosma, M., *'Bijna geen uitweg mogelijk'. Het oorlogsdagboek van Gerlof Verweij over het lot van de joden* (unpublished BA-dissertation Universiteit Leiden, 2008) 25-26.

28 Boom, B. van der, *'Wij weten niets van hun lot'. Gewone Nederlanders en de Holocaust* (Amsterdam 2012) 170-173.

29 Boom, Van der, *Wij weten niets van hun lot*, 79-82.
30 Ibidem, 212.
31 Voet, J., 'De Joodse Raad', NIOD, Doc II 366a, 105.
32 Boom, Van der, *Wij weten niets van hun lot*, 369.
33 Ibidem, 370.
34 Ibidem, 396.

Jewish identity card stamped with a J.

Comparing the persecution of the Jews in the Netherlands, France and Belgium, 1940-1945: similarities, differences, causes[1]
by Pim Griffioen and Ron Zeller

1. Introduction

With regard to the percentage of Jewish victims and survivors during the Shoah, France and the Netherlands are each other's counterpart: 25 per cent of the about 320,000 Jews in France did not survive the persecution, whereas in the Netherlands this was 75 per cent of the 140,000 Jews. Belgium is in between: of the about 66,000 Jews some 40 per cent did not survive. The central question in our book is: what were the *main* causes of the striking differences in Jewish victimization in these three Western European countries?[2]

For an explanation of these national differences it is essential to employ a comparative method regarding the many data that are scattered among the vast body of research literature and primary sources. Based on an explicit periodization and a distinction between three groups in each of the countries – the Occupiers, the National or local factors, and the Jewish population – we have distinguished *comparison factors* for each period and group. These factors are directly or potentially relevant to explain the national differences and thus answer the central research question.[3]

On the one hand, we have carried out in our book an evenly balanced, detailed description, analysis and comparison of the persecution in the three countries. When it comes to comparing, this means *three* comparisons: France–the Netherlands, France–Belgium and Belgium–the Netherlands. On the other hand, in this paper, we search for causes for the high percentage of victims in the Netherlands: the highest in Western Europe in both absolute and relative terms.

2. Comparability

France, Belgium and the Netherlands are well comparable, because the initial situation at the beginning of the German occupation, in May 1940, was similar in many respects.

Looking at the Germans, their occupation policy was aimed at maintaining order, the smooth integration of the national economies into the German war effort and co-operation with the native government bureaucracy. This differed from German occupation policy in Eastern Europe, first and foremost Poland, where native authorities were brutally brushed aside. In Poland, the war was continued against the subjected civilian population and economic exploitation was direct plunder.

National factors there were quite similar as well: all three countries had been parliamentary democracies with a liberal tradition. This contrasted with Germany after 1932 and countries in Eastern Europe. Before the Second World War, no legal distinction was made between Jewish and non-Jewish citizens of France, Belgium and the Netherlands. This was the result of almost 150 years of emancipation and integration. There was some native anti-Semitism in each of the countries, but unlike Nazi Germany and many countries in Eastern Europe, this local anti-Semitism did not result in official discrimination or agitation by the authorities before 1940. Also the percentage of Jews in France, Belgium and the Netherlands before the war did not differ much. It was very low: Jews accounted for three quarters of a per cent of the Belgian and French population, and, 1.5 per cent of the Dutch. The Polish situation, for example, was quite different: more than ten per cent of the total pre-war population was Jewish.

3. Similarities and differences during the beginning of the occupation

3.1 Occupier
From the summer of 1940 onwards, the German rulers used a domination concept in their occupation policy in all three countries. Tempo-

rary, supervisory occupation administrations were established, in German the so-called *Aufsichtsverwaltung*. They left the daily, routine affairs to the local government bureaucracies in each of the three countries as much as possible.[4]

The situation in France differed from the other two countries. Unlike the Netherlands and Belgium, a large part of France remained *unoccupied* after the French military defeat. According to the armistice of June 1940 France continued to exist as a state; the French government moved to the town of Vichy in the so-called Free Zone, about 300 kilometres south of Paris.

A second difference regarding the occupier was the type of administration: unlike Belgium and the occupied part of France, in the Netherlands a *civilian* occupation administration was established, the *Reichskommissariat*, much like in Norway a month before. In the Netherlands this SS and Party-dominated civilian administration was headed by the Austrian Nazi Arthur Seyss-Inquart, who had played a crucial role in the annexation of Austria by Germany in 1938. Both Norway and the Netherlands were considered as regions with 'Germanic' peoples that should become part of the German Reich in the future.[5]

In Belgium and France on the other hand, the German army prevailed in the power struggle with the Party and SS about control over the occupied territories. In these countries, *military* administrations were established, since they served as a springboard for the intended attack on England.[6]

A direct consequence of the civilian occupation regime in the Netherlands and of Hitler's Nazification-order was that leading figures were appointed with a strong ideological background: both Reich-commissioner Seyss-Inquart and the four general-commissioners were all confirmed Nazis. One of them, Hanns Albin Rauter, was also appointed Higher SS and Police Leader (HSSPF). He had been active in the November pogrom of 1938 in Germany. In his position in the Netherlands, Rauter received direct orders from the highest chief of the German Police and SS, Himmler – even by-passing Seyss-Inquart. In short: Nazi ideology was an integral part of the occupation structure in the Netherlands.[7]

In both Belgium and France the military occupation regime was headed by a general. In Belgium the most prominent figure was the chief of the Administration Staff, Eggert Reeder. Although a Nazi Party member, and even holding a rank in the SS, it was clear from the beginning that in his policy Army interests prevailed over SS or Party interests. Especially the SS wanted – as in Germany – full control over the police and security matters. Unlike in the Netherlands, there was no institutional position in Belgium for Nazi Party or SS agencies. Maintaining order and integration of the national economy in the German war efforts were the most important goals for the military administration.[8] In France there was also a military administration, headed by a general. However, a prominent figure in the military top echelon was Werner Best, a legal expert, a convinced Nazi and a high-ranking SS officer. Moreover, Otto Abetz, a Nazi Party activist who represented the German Ministry of Foreign Affairs was sent to Paris. He would become ambassador in Paris and play an important role in negotiations with the French government.[9]

Summarizing, in the Netherlands Nazi ideology was an integral part of the occupation regime; in France this was less the case; in Belgium Nazi ideology played an even lesser role in the occupation regime than in France.

3.2 National and local factors

In contrast to France, where the government remained in power in the so-called 'Free Zone', in the Netherlands and Belgium the government ministers went into exile in May 1940. The top civil servants of the ministries, the so-called Secretaries-general, had received orders from their government to stay in office and co-operate with the occupying force. The two countries had been cut off from the world overseas and to keep the economy running, they depended on Germany. There was another reason for the local authorities to stay in office. They wanted to prevent the native Fascist parties – such as the NSB in the Netherlands and VNV and Rex in Belgium – from gaining government power. In all three countries trade and industry, and numerous organizations in society adapted to the new circumstances in the summer of 1940. It seemed that Germany could no longer lose the war; its domination over the European continent seemed permanent. The majority of the populations adapted to the circumstances, awaiting the further developments and striving to resume daily life as much as possible.[10]

3.3 Jewish populations

The Jewish populations varied considerably in size, nationality and organization. There was no majority consensus on their Jewish identity in any of the three countries. There were numerous economic, social, cultural and religious differences and internal conflicts. The long-established Jewish communities were integrated in society and partly assimilated, especially in the Netherlands and France. In the Netherlands, the great majority of the Jews had been fully integrated citizens for generations. In Belgium, however, more than 90 per cent of the Jews were Eastern European immigrants. The majority had arrived in the 1920s, followed by refugees from Germany in 1930s. They were *not* integrated in society and were mainly considered outsiders. Again, the situation in France was more indefinite. Like in the Netherlands, there was a large group of integrated, partly assimilated Jews, though there was a similarly sized group of refugees and immigrants without French citizenship.[11]

4. Anti-Jewish policies, summer 1940 – summer 1942

Within only a few months after the beginning of the German occupation the first decrees against Jews were issued in all three countries. This anti-Jewish policy had a mainly *administrative* character: decrees and measures that were issued aimed at *gradually* excluding the Jews from society and the economy. At first, no violent actions against the Jews or massive arrests were carried out. In this respect, Western Europe differed from occupied Poland and other East European areas, where a policy of terror and forced 'ghettoization' was carried out from the outset.[12]

In France the newly formed Vichy-government initiated its own anti-

Jewish policy. In certain respects, this French policy was even more radical than the German policy. Moreover, the French laws against the Jews were enforced in both the occupied and the 'Free Zone', whereas the German decrees were valid solely in the occupied area.

The French anti-Jewish policy can be explained only against the background of the severe military defeat of France and the resulting collapse of the French Third Republic. This generated a profound change in French politics and society, originating in the 1930s. There was a growing unease over the deep economic crisis, the poor functioning of the democratic system and the large numbers of foreigners and refugees, among whom were many Jews.[13]

The new French Cabinet was headed by Marshal Philippe Pétain, who had been appointed shortly before the armistice of June 1940. With the consent of a majority in Parliament, he abolished the democratic system. Pétain became head of state (*Chef de l'État*) and received sweeping powers to rule the country. With the exception of Minister Pierre Laval, the Vichy-government consisted of hardly any politicians from the previous Third Republic. State power passed mainly into the hands of former top civil servants and other technocrats, who now became Cabinet Ministers. This regime was bent on maximum autonomy for France in a German-dominated Europe and opted for a policy of collaboration (*politique de collaboration*) with the occupying force. The regime launched a nationalistic, corporatist and xenophobic domestic program: the 'National Revolution' (*Révolution Nationale*). Authority, family values, patriotism and traditional Catholic principles were to be reinforced by legislation, education, church authorities, the civil service and local notables. French society would no longer have room for certain groups: Freemasons, Communists, other political dissidents, foreigners and Jews. The anti-Semitism of the German occupier offered an opportunity for an independent, rival *French* policy of excluding the Jews, which affected not only Jewish immigrants, but also the Jewish Frenchmen themselves.[14]

In the occupied part of France, and in Belgium and the Netherlands alike, the Nazis actively incorporated the local civil service into the preparation of anti-Jewish decrees and their implementation. In the Netherlands and Belgium the highest civil servants expressed objections at first, and referred to the Constitution and the International Convention on War (The Hague, 1907). Law did not allow discrimination on the basis of race or religion. But under German pressure, the top civil servants began to co-operate.[15] Comparison shows that anti-Jewish policies in all three countries were implemented with astonishing speed: in as little as three months after the national armies' defeat the beginning of social and economic segregation of the Jewish populations – with the co-operation of the native bureaucracies – was a fact, directly affecting more than half a million people. Despite the very recent military hostilities, material damage, chaos and the moving about of large numbers of refugees, as well as the severe mental shock of the quick, total defeat among both authorities and the populations, the native government bureaucracies were able and sufficiently disposed to co-operate in the implementation of decrees against the Jews.

How did public opinion respond to the anti-Jewish policies in the three countries? Unlike in France and Belgium, there were public protests against the first anti-Jewish decrees of autumn 1940 and early 1941 in the Netherlands. Churches, university professors and students protested against the Jews being banned from civil service and other public offices. Petitions were presented and students went on strike. But the occupier ignored them and closed down the universities.[16]

In the first months of 1941, tension rose in the Netherlands. Riots, provoked by Dutch National-Socialists in Amsterdam – secretly supported by local German authorities, led to German intervention: on February 12, the old Jewish quarter was fenced with barbed-wire, and a Jewish council, much like in occupied Poland during the winter of 1939-1940, was installed. After further incidents the German SS and Police chief in Holland, Rauter, in consultation with his superiors Seyss-Inquart and Himmler, ordered a reprisal roundup of more than 400 young Jewish men in Amsterdam. The action was carried out in public with brute force by German police, with many non-Jewish witnesses. This violent German action provoked a general protest strike in Amsterdam and surrounding towns, organized by the underground Communist Party. The two-day strike took the German authorities by surprise. On its second day, German police troops, under the personal supervision of Rauter, put down the strike with brute force: killing nine people, wounding dozens and arresting more than a hundred people of whom 18 were later executed. The enclosure of the Jewish quarter was only temporary, the barbed-wire was removed; a ghetto was not imposed. But the Jewish Council (the German term: *Judenrat*) remained. Almost all of the about 400 Jews who had been rounded up were deported to German concentration camps, most notably Mauthausen in Austria, and with the exception of one, none of them survived.[17]

It is important to stress the various mainly unintended consequences, of the first brutal roundup of Jews, the February Strike and its violent suppression, not only for the further policy pursued by the occupier, but also for the local authorities, the non-Jewish and Jewish populations. This was the first time in the occupied Netherlands that the German regime acted publicly and forcibly against the Jewish fellow-citizens. In Belgium, the shock of a first public, violent roundup and deportation of Jews would take place much later, in August 1942, at the beginning of the general, massive deportations, and shortly after the introduction of the Jewish badge.[18] In France, Jews were rounded up in the streets for the first time in August 1941. This action, however, was carried out by the French police in Paris, *not* the Germans, and the victims were almost all refugees and immigrants without French citizenship. They were detained in French internment camps.[19]

The German rulers realized that brute force against the Jews in public should be avoided because, clearly, this could lead to serious unrest and economic damage. To prevent this from happening again, the on-going exclusion, isolation and spoliation of the Jewish population became a matter of administration, regulations and deception. A sham 'bank' was established to rob the Jews of their assets and savings.[20] New, incidental reprisal roundups of Jews were carried out in June 1941 in Amsterdam and in the autumn of the same year in the East of the country. Now, German police enlisted the Dutch local police to help in carrying out these arrests under false pretences, such as 'interrogation'. In reality, however, all Jewish men seized were sent to the concentration camp of Mauthausen in Austria, where all of them were killed shortly after arrival. Their relatives in the Netherlands were informed that their fathers and brothers had died on account of ill-health, pneumonia, etc. Because of this, it was soon well known among the Jewish population that 'Mauthausen' meant certain death. This had a very intimidating effect for a long time: from spring 1941 until about the end of 1942.[21]

During the months following the strike, decision-making and preparation of new anti-Jewish decrees and measures became more and more an *exclusively* German matter, increasingly directed on a *local* level. Most of the top Dutch civil servants, who had to deal directly with the occupier, resigned or were dismissed – albeit not explicitly over the persecution of the Jews – and were replaced by pro-German figures appointed by Seyss-Inquart. The Jews were ultimately removed from the Dutch authorities' control. This situation was much the same in Belgium. However, in both countries the native civil service remained involved in the implementation, for example in sending Jewish men to labour camps in the spring of 1942. In the Netherlands these camps were mainly in the north and east of the country, in Belgium these men were sent to camps in Northern France along the Channel coast.[22] In France, on the other hand, there were *continuing* contacts and negotiations between German and French authorities on the *national* level regarding decision-making in anti-Jewish policy.[23]

For the non-Jewish population in the Netherlands the ferocious suppression of the February Strike had a deterrent effect on any further public protest or opposition. It was clear that the strike did not in any way delay or mitigate the on-going persecution. From then on, anti-German sentiments were expressed in the growing clandestine press.[24]

The responses to the persecution of the Jews in 1940-1941 among the populations in France and Belgium, were mainly characterized by passivity and indifference.[25] In Belgium, where more than 90 per cent of the Jews were foreigners, not Belgians, the persecution actually became visible with the introduction of the Jewish badge in early June 1942. In

France half of the Jewish population was not French, but immigrant and refugee. Like in Belgium, the first real shock in public opinion regarding the persecution was the introduction of the Jewish badge in June 1942, soon followed by the beginning of the deportations.[26]

On the eve of the massive deportations in July 1942, the position of the Jews in the three countries varied. This had to do with the nature of the central organizations that had been imposed upon the Jews in 1941, like the Amsterdam Jewish Council. This council, lacking any formal status, was used in the implementation of all kinds of measures. It was subjected to German civilian and police authorities in Amsterdam solely on the *local* level, and this remained so even after the council's authority spread nation-wide in the autumn of 1941. In Belgium and France, the German police did not attain full control over these organizations. In Belgium, the German Security Police had to share its grip on the imposed Jewish organization – the *Association des Juifs en Belgique* (AJB) – with various subdivisions of the military administration and the Belgian ministry of the Interior, thus on the *national* level. In France, the similar organization – called *Union Générale des Israélites de France* (UGIF) – was formally even solely subordinate to French authorities, not to the German occupier. Moreover, the UGIF was in fact divided into two branches, one in the occupied North, and one in the unoccupied South. The differences in the nature, subordination, and official assignment of Jewish imposed organizations were telling of the position of the Jewish populations in the three countries, more than the character or personality of the Jewish leaders involved in them.[27]

So far, we have mentioned some aspects of anti-Jewish policy during the first two years of occupation, until the beginning of the deportations. For the second two years – 1942 to 1944 – we shall again look first at the German occupiers who organized the deportations, followed by National or local factors, and the Jewish populations.

5. Deportations, hiding and escape, summer 1942 – autumn 1944

5.1 *Planning and organization*

Three factors were of major importance in the implementation of the deportations: 1) the transport opportunities or availability of trains; 2) the size of the available police forces; and 3) the relative freedom of action of the German police agencies directly involved, especially the anti-Jewish section within the German Security Police in the three countries. How and when did these factors influence the difference in the percentage of Jews deported from France, Belgium and the Netherlands?

Concerning the transport opportunities it should first of all be noted that Adolf Eichmann in Berlin, who organized the deportations to Poland, looked at France, Belgium and the Netherlands as a whole when it came to ordering German trains. After some changes, in late June 1942, he planned for 40,000 French Jews, 10,000 Belgian and 40,000 Jews from the Netherlands. German trains were available for deportations.[28]

The second factor was the availability of the police apparatus in the three countries. In France the occupier had some 2,400 Security Police and 5,000 Order Police; a moderate amount for a vast country like France. Therefore, since the beginning of the occupation, the German police commanders co-operated with the French police in maintaining order and fighting their common enemy: the resistance, especially the Communist underground movement.[29]

The French government in Vichy strove for maximum autonomy in the occupied part. It aimed to avoid direct German interventions as much as possible. In May 1942, a Higher SS and Police Leader (HSSPF) was appointed in occupied France. From now on, both in France and in the Netherlands there was a German SS and Police chief with full control over German police matters, including the deportations of Jews. In this respect, the military administration in France no longer played any significant role. Therefore, in negotiations in early July 1942, the highest German SS and police commanders in France – Karl Oberg and Helmut Knochen – made the condition that more autonomy for the French police in the occupied zone would *only* be possible when they co-operated to great extent in deporting the Jews. The French government and head of the French police, René Bousquet, were willing to do this – even in the unoccupied zone – but only in the case of foreign and stateless Jews. The Germans agreed, since they could at least start the mass deportations. After this German-French agreement of early July 1942, the German police commanders' personnel problem had been solved for the time being: 100,000 French policemen, of whom some 30,000 were in the Paris region, had become available for roundups and deportations of Jews.[30]

In Belgium the occupier had a total of some 1,800 own policemen. Most of these were Military Police, directly subordinate to the Military Administration, and not to SS commanders as was the case in the Netherlands and France. On the other hand, however, General Reeder's military police was willing to cooperate in arresting and rounding up Jews for deportation. The Military Administration also needed this police for other tasks, such as guarding German objects and fighting Belgian resistance.[31]

In the Netherlands, the supreme German SS commander of police, Rauter, had a total of about 4,700 German police personnel. In addition, he could also use the Dutch police. In the course of about two years, Rauter had reorganized and centralized the Dutch regular police, and made it in fact a state-police, subordinate only to him. The authority over the Dutch police had been removed from the mayors and also from the Dutch ministry of the Interior. Only in the Netherlands the indigenous police organization had been made subordinate directly to the occupier.[32] For example, in Amsterdam, counting 60 per cent of the Dutch Jewish population, the city police was headed by a chief-commissioner who was an NSB-member and who had been appointed by Rauter, after the 1941 February Strike. The Amsterdam police had some 2,600 personnel and their chief-commissioner was eager to offer his services to the occupier.[33]

In all three countries a sufficiently extensive police force could be used to arrest and deport the Jews. The third factor – the degree of autonomy of the German agencies directly involved – can only be measured by examining the sequence of the deportations in the three countries.

5.2 First phase of deportations, July – mid-November 1942

The first roundups and large-scale deportations in France started in mid-July 1942 with carefully prepared mass roundups in the Paris region, carried out by the French *regular* police, using lists with names and addresses taken from French files. Jews had been registered in 1941. From the beginning of August roundups and arrests also took place in the unoccupied part of France, at first from internment camps, soon also from cities. All actions were brutally carried out by French police, separating families, while a lot of non-Jews witnessed the events. These first deportations, that included women, old people, children, and even French citizen children born in France of immigrant parents, generated a lot of unease and protests in French society, especially in the unoccupied South of the country. Church leaders and organizations for humanitarian assistance protested and tried to intervene with the French authorities. Behind the scenes, there was American political and diplomatic pressure on the French government in Vichy. Under the influence of all these responses, Pétain and Laval decided in early September 1942 to temporarily cease large-scale arrests of Jews. They did not want to lose what was left of their political support in society. Now, French authorities and police would limit themselves to inconspicuous, small-scale arrests of Jews with specific foreign nationalities, and individual arrests of trespassers of anti-Jewish regulations. All arrested Jews were taken by the French Railways to the transit camp Drancy at the outskirts of Paris. This camp was administered and guarded by French police. From there, German trains deported the Jews to Auschwitz and other death camps in Poland.[34]

In Belgium and the Netherlands large-scale deportations of Jews, which also started in July, continued not only in August, but also in September and October 1942. In Belgium and the Netherlands, at first, individually addressed, written call-up orders were issued by the German Security Police to force the Jews to transit camps, before deporting them to what was called 'employment in the East under police supervision'. At first, many Jews who received these written summonses failed to report in both Belgium and the Netherlands.[35] Because of this, the German police had to change to other methods. In Belgium, from mid-August 1942, German military police was used to carry out roundups and street arrests in Antwerp and Brussels, where about 90 per cent of all Belgian Jews lived. Despite the registration data with names and addresses available to the German police, these actions as well as individual arrests were carried out brutally and in public. Only Jewish immigrants and refugees, who made up more than 90 per cent of all Jews in Belgium, were arrested. In Antwerp, the local German Security Police forced the city police to assist in the arresting of Jews in August. The transit-camp for Jews was in an army barracks in the town of Malines, situated right in between Brussels and Antwerp. In the Netherlands, after the written summons failed to generate a sufficient response, German police carried out some small-scale roundups that were designed to intimidate: the Jews taken prisoner were held hostage to force those who had received call-up orders to report. Repeatedly, German police warned that Jews who did not report, or went into hiding, would be arrested and taken away straight to Mauthausen concentration camp as punishment. Compared to this, Westerbork transit camp and the so-called 'work in the East' seemed the lesser of two evils. The risk of going into hiding and being caught was estimated much higher than the risks involved in going to a labour camp in Poland.[36] Although some Jews reported and many of the hostages were indeed released, the results remained insufficient. Instead of large-scale roundups like in Belgium, German police in the Netherlands turned to house-to-house arrests after the evening curfew, starting at the beginning of September 1942.[37]

In both Belgium and France, predominantly Eastern European Jews were targeted in roundups. This played a leading role in the responses and in the setting up of Jewish self-help and underground organizations. As a result of the first big roundups in public, the remaining Jews were in fact encouraged to opt for illegality, to go into hiding, to obtain false IDs, to move or to make an attempt to cross the border and escape to Switzerland or Spain.[38]

Different from the violent actions in public in France and Belgium, in the Netherlands the house-to-house arrests were carried out in the evening, *after* the beginning of the curfew. The roundups of February 1941 had led to a protest strike in Amsterdam, so this time the German police tried to avoid public violence that could again lead to serious public unrest. They now employed various methods of intimidation (Mauthausen) and deception.

In the Netherlands, shortly after the beginning of the deportations a policy of temporary exemptions was adopted by the German police and other German agencies. In the autumn of 1942 about 46,000 Jews – or one-third of the remaining Jews in Holland – could make use of these opportunities. This created a lot of anxiety among the Jewish population and hastened demoralization. For months, the exemptions offered many opportunities to temporarily escape deportation, but by the end of 1942 the first exemptions were abolished. Then gradually most exemptions were abolished, and those with still valid exemptions, who stayed at their legal addresses, were arrested.[39]

In Amsterdam, during September 1942, it was mainly the local, *regular* police receiving orders from their pro-German chief-commissioner to arrest Jews. However, this happened reluctantly, with growing aversion and Rauter was soon dissatisfied with the results. Within a week, the chief-commissioner was compelled to use members of the so-called Amsterdam Police Battalion (PBA). The about 250 members of this unit had received a pro-German, national-socialist police training in 1941 and early 1942. After the chief-commissioner fell seriously ill at the beginning of October 1942 – he died a few weeks later – the local German police commander had to use other units for arresting the Jews and tracing Jews who had gone into hiding. These units received their instructions directly from the German police; they consisted of members of the aforementioned Police Battalion, members of the Voluntary Auxiliary Police, the Amsterdam branch of which consisted of 200 men, and other pro-German, Nazified groups and individuals. All men were members of the NSB and/or members of the Dutch SS. From about mid-September and early October 1942, in Amsterdam and other big cities (except The Hague), where more than three-quarters of all Dutch Jews lived, the normal, regular Dutch police no longer arrested Jews for deportation. Instead, this was done by small, special units of German police and Dutch National-Socialists, under *direct* German supervision.[40]

The high percentage of Jews that was deported from the Netherlands, compared with Belgium and France in this first phase, can largely be explained by the fact that the order was given by the chief of German police and SS in Holland for the evacuation of the Jewish labour camps in the North and East of the country, where Jewish men had been sent to since the beginning of 1942. At first only unemployed had been sent there, later also men who still had a job or a business. After the beginning of the deportations in July the impression arose that it was better to be put to work in the Netherlands, than to be sent to labour camps in Poland. However, in early October 1942 *all* Jewish men in the Dutch camps, and their families outside, were taken to Westerbork Transit Camp. Altogether, it concerned more than 12,000 people. Almost all of them were sent to Auschwitz that same month. In one blow 12 per cent of the total of deported Jews was thus taken away at once. This was the highest monthly number ever reached in the Netherlands.[41]

In contrast, in France and Belgium the anti-Jewish sections of the German Security Police, who had to organize the deportations, were restricted in their freedom of action by their own superiors for political reasons. In France the obstacles were severest. The SS-superiors of the German police in France curtailed their own anti-Jewish experts because they had also other interests, such as the general co-operation with the French police leadership in maintaining public order, and the struggle against French resistance. The highest German police chiefs also had to take into account the very significant economic contribution of France to the German war effort.[42]

In Belgium, the German police indeed gained control over the deportations of the Jews, like in the Netherlands, but it had no sizeable police force at its disposal that could be used at all times. Nor did the German police have full control over the forced organization that had been imposed upon the Jewish population. In the Netherlands, on the other hand, the German police did have full control over police matters and over the imposed Jewish organization, the Amsterdam Jewish Council.

When comparing the deportations in France and the Netherlands until mid-November 1942, a first observation is that in France the absolute numbers were higher than in the Netherlands, but proportionately France had fallen behind the Netherlands with 10 per cent of the total Jewish populations in the two countries. In France, this difference was caused by the anti-Jewish section's lack of freedom to act within the German police, and the refusal of the French government to continue with large-scale arrests of Jews in September 1942. Because of this, the anti-Jewish section that organized the deportations could not utilize any of the 30 trains that had already been made available to France for October 1942. Would it have been possible to use these trains according to the German plan, the deportation percentage for France would have been nearly equal to the Netherlands by mid-November 1942, 23 per cent, instead of the real French quota of 13 per cent. The *peak* of the deportations from the evacuated labour camps in Holland in October 1942 and the *simultaneous stagnation* in France explain the difference between these two countries before the middle of November 1942.[43]

In Belgium the roundups of August and September 1942, as mentioned, soon also had a counter-productive effect for the German organizers. The remaining Jews refused to wear the Jewish badge any longer; they sold their furniture, tried to obtain false identity papers, and tried to hide or escape. Because of this, by the end of October 1942, there was a permanent downswing in the deportations. Only after this stagnation had already started, a shortage of German trains for further deportations of Jews from Belgium arose during the winter months of 1942-1943. This shortage was caused by military transports to the Eastern Front. But in January 1943, when gradually more Jews had been seized by individual arrests, deportation trains were made available again for Belgium.[44]

In Belgium, the German occupiers announced the general labour draft for Belgians in factories in Germany in early October 1942. This caused a shock wave in Belgian society. Many Belgians tried to evade compulsory labour and they received a lot of support from their fellow-countrymen. This German measure was an important impetus for the rise of organized resistance, hiding and escape networks in Belgium. Jews could profit from these opportunities; many Belgians now realized what the threat of persecution and deportation, which Jews had already experienced, really meant. Compulsory labour in Germany was introduced in September-October 1942 in Belgium as well as in France. In the Netherlands on the other hand, similar more extensive organized hiding opportunities would emerge much later: after the great protest strikes of late April-early May 1943, when the compulsory labour in Germany was severely stepped up in the Netherlands as well.[45]

5.3 Second phase of deportations, mid-November 1942 – July 1943
In October 1942, the Jewish labour camps in the Netherlands were evacuated. During the first months of 1943, Jewish hospitals, homes for the elderly, mental institutions and orphanages were raided and their occupants evacuated. It concerned about 8,000 Jews.[46] Along with the Jewish labour camp inmates more than 20,000 Jews were thus deported from places of isolation and concentration where they had been an easy target for the German police. This accounts for almost 20 per cent of the total deportation figure in the Netherlands. In Belgium, on the other hand, at this stage deportations from Jewish orphanages and homes for the elderly, administered by the AJB, were postponed by the Military Administration. From October 1942 until the end of the German occupation of Belgium all emphasis in the persecution was on tracing of Jews in hiding. It had become clear that the German police had lost their grip on most of the remaining Jews in Belgium. The Military Administration reported in December 1942 to Berlin: 'The Jews that are still in the country are concealed in such a manner that further transports will prove to be very difficult'.[47]

The German police in the Netherlands set up a second transit-camp for Jews in January 1943. For months it was deliberately presented not as a transit camp, but as a 'reception camp' (*Auffanglager*) for permanent labour in various large-scale industries. However, in reality also this camp Vught facilitated isolation and concentration and it served as a transit camp from the beginning. In almost all cases the prisoners were not sent directly to Poland, but first to the Westerbork transit camp, and from there to the death camps.[48]

The German police in the Netherlands used different tactics to keep the deportations moving, such as the already mentioned temporary exemptions from deportation which were withdrawn step by step, the on-going evacuations to Amsterdam, concentration in three city districts there, followed by big roundups in these districts from May to September 1943. All this enabled the German police to carry out the deportation of more than 34,000 Jews to the Sobibor extermination camp in Poland, between early March and late July 1943. Only 18 of them would survive.[49]

These surreptitious, cunning, coherent methods were employed by the German Security Police in the Netherlands, commanded by Wilhelm Harster from the summer of 1940 to September 1943.[50] In Belgium and occupied France, such methods were not employed. A major reason for this difference was the fact that only in the Netherlands by July 1942 the German police had attained an almost unlimited control over the organization of the deportations. Because of this freedom of action it had the opportunity to develop and implement methods of its own interest and design.

In early November 1942, the Allied forces landed in French North Africa. German troops now crossed the demarcation line of unoccupied Southern France and Italian troops occupied the South-Eastern part of the country. The 'Free Zone' where the French Vichy government had its seat was now occupied. The terms of the French-German armistice of June 1940 formally remained in force, the French government stayed in office, a German occupation administration in the south was not established, and a formal distinction between the two zones was maintained. But in reality everything changed. German police now also got access to Southern France.[51]

After some small-scale arrests during the winter months, French police carried out a larger scale roundup in the Paris region and the rest of the country in mid-February 1943. This was the first big roundup since the summer of 1942. As a result, the German police was able to deport some 7,000 Jews from France in February and March 1943. But to the anti-Jewish section of the German police in France it was clear that further deportations would only be possible when French police arrested more Jews and when the French government stripped the citizenship of Jewish immigrants who had received French passports shortly before the Second World War. In this way – according to the German-French police agreement of July 1942 – these Jews would immediately be arrested and deported, before these Jews would have a direct reason to go into hiding. However, German-French negotiations over this issue dragged on for months. Ultimately, in September 1943, head of state Pétain decided that the necessary French law would not be issued. This decision was prompted by the course of the war against Germany and by the fear of new, widespread reactions and protests.[52]

In addition to this, in the South-Eastern part of France, controlled by Italian troops, the French authorities and police wanted to hand over foreign Jews for deportation to the Germans. But the Italian military authorities prevented them from doing this. In general, the Italians refused to hand over any of the 25,000 to 30,000 Jews in their zone of occupation.[53]

Thus the ambitious deportation plans, drafted by the anti-Jewish section of the German police in March 1943 came to nothing. Despite the availability of plenty of German trains in the spring of 1943, between the end of March and late June that year, not a single deportation train with Jews left France. If the plan[54] for April, May and June of 1943, for which sufficient trains and internment camp capacity were available, had been implemented, the total number of deportees would not have differed much from the Netherlands. The anti-Jewish section in the German police was again curtailed by its own SS superiors for political reasons.

5.4 Third phase of deportations, July 1943 – September 1944

During the third and last phase of the deportations, after the last Sobibor transports of July 1943, the deportation rate in the Netherlands decreased to a level that did not differ much from France's. The last roundups in Amsterdam took place at the end of September 1943, after which the Jewish Council and any legally organized Jewish community life ceased to exist. In France, after Vichy's rejection of the denaturalization law, the German police, backed by SS-chief Himmler in Germany, now decided to make an end to the German-French collaboration policy regarding the Jews. Instead, the German police organized roundups and manhunts independent of the French authorities. So it was only in the autumn of 1943 – and especially from December – that the anti-Jewish section of the German police finally received a freedom of action like their Dutch colleagues had since the very beginning of the deportations in July 1942.

Eichmann's special representative, Alois Brunner, was sent to France with a small team of experienced SS officers. He formed special squads that included members of small, radical French fascist parties and other pro-Nazi elements, but *not* the French regular police. Jews were no longer safe, including those Jews who until then had not been deported on a large scale, such as Jews with French citizenship and war veterans. The same applied to the Jews in the Italian Zone in the South-East of France, which was occupied by German troops in September 1943, two months after the fall of dictator Mussolini.[55]

Despite the freedom of action, the German police failed to accomplish really large-scale deportations. First, the size of available German police remained limited; in other words: only now the lack of German manpower became manifest. Second, in the formerly unoccupied zone – now called 'Southern Zone' – the Jewish badge had never been introduced. Third, since the occupation of Southern France and the introduction of compulsory labour of Frenchmen in Germany in October-November 1942, French resistance and organized networks for hiding and escape had grown to a large extent. Fourth, there was an extended network of Jewish self-help organizations, both legal and illegal, that co-operated with the French resistance, church-people, and French and foreign legal organizations for humanitarian aid. This last factor also played a considerable role in Belgium where Jewish immigrants – both Communists and Zionists – set up a joint underground network in September 1942 in co-operation with the Belgian resistance organization Independence Front. In Antwerp, however, this development went slower, because Jews who could organize resistance and underground networks had gone to Brussels shortly before the deportations began. Moreover, in the Antwerp region members of the Flemish SS were more active in tracing Jews in hiding. The victimization rate in Antwerp was thus higher than in Brussels.[56]

During the last year of occupation in France, until the liberation in late August 1944, the German police was able to organize about one to two trains with Jewish deportees every month. During this last phase almost 24,000 Jews were seized and deported. Although the absolute numbers of deportees in France and the Netherlands did not differ very much during this last phase, in France they represented a lower percentage of the total Jewish population.

Of the about 320,000 Jews in France on the eve of the Second World War, about 80,000 did not survive. Approximately 24,500 of them were French citizens; the majority of the victims were immigrants and refugees. This was mainly caused by the German-French police agreement of early July 1942 that remained in effect until about September 1943.[57] In Belgium the great majority of 25,000 victims were immigrants and refugees as well. The main cause here was the fact that only about 4,000 of the 66,000 Jews in Belgium had Belgian citizenship and they were exempted from deportation by the Military Administration until early September 1943.[58] In contrast with Belgium and France, in the Netherlands the distinction between native and foreign Jews in chances of survival has not been of similar significance; Jews with Dutch citizenship were deported from the outset.

When considering the precise role of the native, regular police in the roundups and deportations of Jews it appears that at least 61 per cent of the 80,000 Jews who did not survive the persecutions in France came into German hands through the French regular police, or died in French internment camps. As for the more than 25,000 Jews deported from Belgium to the Nazi death camps, the Belgian authorities and regular police were directly involved with about 4,300 Jews, or 17 per cent, mostly from the Antwerp region. All others were seized by German police, other German agencies and/or with the help of Belgian individual denouncers and pro-German collaborators. Of the approximately 107,000 Jews deported from the Netherlands, about 26,000, or 24 per cent, were arrested exclusively or mainly by Dutch regular police (municipal police in cities, *maréchaussee* in the countryside). More than 80,000 Jews were seized by other forces or in another way, i.e., by written call-up orders, the German Order Police, German Security Police, newly trained pro-German units under German command and other pro-Nazi denouncers who often received financial rewards for tracing hidden Jews. This 7 per cent difference between the regular local police in Belgium and the Netherlands does not account decisively for the ultimate and much larger difference of 35 per cent in the victimization rate between these two countries.[59]

6. Conclusions

The main causes of the divergence between the Netherlands and France were partly different from the causes of the divergence between the Netherlands and Belgium. Most striking in the case of France is that the Vichy government – because of its close collaboration with the occupying force – facilitated extensive deportations in the summer of 1942. The Vichy government was also responsible for the interruption of the deportations in the autumn of that year and from March to June 1943, when the anti-Jewish section of the German Security Police was restricted by its own SS superiors. The German Security Police in the Netherlands, however, could make full use of its freedom of action. These factors also mainly explain the difference between France and Belgium: the role of the Vichy government on the one hand, and the relatively larger freedom of action for the German Security Police and its helpers in Belgium on the other.

When comparing Belgium and the Netherlands, we can conclude that an explanation for the difference can be given by the method of violent roundups and arrests, in public, in Belgium in the summer of 1942. This stimulated the remaining Jews to go underground at a relatively early stage, whereas in the Netherlands the German police, because of its greater freedom of action, could organize the deportations much more methodically, with less public violence. This was partly the result of the 1941 February strike after which the occupiers realized that the use of force against the Jewish Dutchmen in public could lead to serious unrest and economic damage. In Belgium, after the early and more radical introduction of compulsory labour in Germany for Belgians in general, organized hiding and escape opportunities materialized eight months earlier than in the Netherlands, which proved a crucial difference in time. Finally, the number and percentage of victims was determined by the way in which the German occupier, especially the German police, continued to use the Amsterdam Jewish Council during the deportations, and the responses among the Jewish population generated by the occupier's methods. These responses were determined by three factors: a) the nature of the German methods which consisted of a combination of intimidation and various forms of deception; b) the weak, informal position of the Jewish Council without any space for negotiating; and c) the largely though not completely assimilated background of the Jewish population in the Netherlands. Because of this, people were inclined to cling to legal options of deferment for a long time. These legal options however, appeared to be part of the deportation system and – in contrast to France and Belgium – counter-acted illegality, such as massive hiding or attempts to escape abroad.

Notes

1   This paper is based on the research and conclusions of our book: *Jodenvervolging in Nederland, Frankrijk en België, 1940-1945: overeenkomsten, verschillen, oorzaken* (The Persecution of the Jews in the Netherlands, France and Belgium, 1940-1945: similarities, differences, causes. Amsterdam: Boom Publishers, September 2011; with an English summary on p. 999-1011).

2   Benz, W. (ed.) (1991/1996²), *Dimension des Völkermords: die Zahl der jüdischen Opfer des Nationalsozialismus* (München: R. Oldenbourg), 15-16, 132-135, 162-165. See also: Griffioen, P. and R. Zeller (1998), 'A Comparative Analysis of the Persecution of the Jews in the Netherlands and Belgium during the Second World War'. In: Lammers, C.J. (ed.), *The Netherlands' Journal of Social Sciences*, vol. 34, no. 2 (Assen: Van Gorcum), 126-164; idem (2006), 'Anti-Jewish Policy and Organization of the Deportations in France and the Netherlands, 1940-1944: A Comparative Study'. In: *Holocaust and Genocide Studies*, vol. 20, no. 3 (Washington D.C./Oxford: USHMM/ Oxford University Press), 437-473.

3   Griffioen & Zeller, *Jodenvervolging*, 73-80, 1000; Lorenz, C. (1997), *Konstruktion der Vergangenheit. Eine Einführung in die Geschichtstheorie* (Cologne/Weimar/Vienna: Böhlau), 231-284, 342.

4   For the term 'herrschaftliche Aufsichtsverwaltung', see: Best, W. (1941), 'Die deutschen Aufsichtsverwaltungen in Frankreich, Belgien, den Niederlanden, Norwegen, Dänemark und im Protektorat Böhmen und Mähren. Vergleichende Übersicht. Manuskript. Nur für den Dienstgebrauch, Stand: Ende August-Anfang September 1941' (Darmstadt: L.C. Wittich), Archives of the Institut für Zeitgeschichte (IfZ): ED 3; also in the Bundes-Archiv Berlin (BAB): T-501, r. 101, fr. 1292-1375. Cf. Friedrich Wimmer, 'Die deutsche Verwaltung in den Niederlanden', lecture delivered in Berlin, October 10, 1940, p. 7; Archives of the Netherlands Institute for War Holocaust and Genocide Studies (NIOD), Amsterdam, archival collection nr. 20: Generalkommissar für Verwaltung und Justiz (VuJ), Stab, 67036-49; cited in: De Jong, L. (1969-1991), *Het Koninkrijk der Nederlanden in de Tweede Wereldoorlog* (14 vols., The Hague/Leiden: Martinus Nijhoff, scholarly ed.), vol. 4 (1972), 66; cf. Romijn, P. (2006), *Burgemeesters in oorlogstijd. Besturen onder Duitse bezetting* (Amsterdam: Balans), 130-132.

5   Kwiet, K. (1968), *Reichskommissariat Niederlande: Versuch und Scheitern nationalsozialistischer Neuordnung* (Stuttgart: Deutsche Verlags-Anstalt), 61-68. Bohn, R. (1997), 'Vorwort', in: Bohn, R. (ed.), *Die deutsche Herrschaft in den 'germanischen' Ländern 1940–1945* (Stuttgart: Franz Steiner), 7-10.

6   Umbreit, H. (1988), 'Auf dem Weg zu Kontinentalherrschaft', in: Kroener, B.R., et al., *Das Deutsche Reich und der Zweite Weltkrieg*, vol. 5: Organisation und Mobilisierung des deutschen Machtbereichs, sub-vol. 5.1: Kriegsverwaltung, Wirtschaft und personelle Ressourcen 1939-1941 (Stuttgart: DVA), 3-345; Röhr, W. (1997), 'System oder organisiertes Chaos? Fragen einer Typologie der deutschen Okkupationsregime im Zweiten Weltkrieg', in: Bohn (ed.), *Die deutsche Herrschaft in den 'germanischen' Ländern*, 11-45.

7   Kwiet, *Reichskommissariat Niederlande*. In 't Veld, N.K.C.A. (1976), *De SS en Nederland. Documenten uit SS-archieven, 1935-1945* (The Hague: Martinus Nijhoff). Griffioen & Zeller, 'A Comparative Analysis of the Persecution', 129-130.

8   Warmbrunn, W. (1993), *The German Occupation of Belgium, 1940-1944* (New York: Lang), 69-70. De Jonghe, A. (1972), *Hitler en het politieke lot van België (1940-1944). De vestiging van een Zivilverwaltung in België en Noord-Frankrijk*, vol. 1 (Antwerp etc.: De Nederlandsche Boekhandel), 23, 64-66, 70-71.

9   Umbreit, H. (1968), *Der Militärbefehlshaber in Frankreich 1940-1944* (Boppard am Rhein: Harald Boldt), 12-32; Herbert, U. (1996), *Best. Biographische Studien über Radikalismus, Weltanschauung und Vernunft 1903-1989* (Bonn: J.H.W. Dietz Nachfolger), 252-256. Fox, J.P. (1992), 'German Bureaucrat or Nazified Ideologue? Ambassador Otto Abetz and Hitler's Anti-Jewish Policies 1940-44', in: Fry, M.G. (ed.), *Power, Personalities and Policies: Essays in Honour of Donald Cameron Watt* (London: Frank Cass), 175-232. Lambauer, B. (2005), 'Opportunistischer Antisemitismus. Der deutsche Botschafter Otto Abetz und die Judenverfolgung in Frankreich (1940-1942)', in: *Vierteljahrshefte für Zeitgeschichte*, vol. 53, no. 2 (Munich: Institute of Contemporary History), 241-273.

10 Hirschfeld, G. (1988), *Nazi Rule and Dutch Collaboration. The Netherlands under German Occupation, 1940–1945* (Oxford etc.: Berg), 57–65. Gérard-Libois, J., Gotovitch, J. (1971), *L'an 40: la Belgique occupée* (Brussels: CRISP), 40, 150-163, 179; Azéma, J.P., Bédarida, F. (eds.) (1993), *La France des années noires*, vol. 1: *De la défaite à Vichy* (Paris: Le Seuil); Burrin, Ph. (1996), *France under the Germans. Collaboration and compromise* (New York: The New Press), 18-31 (chapter 2: 'An undecided present').

11 Israel, J.I., R. Salverda (eds.) (2002), *Dutch Jewry. Its history and secular culture (1500-2000)* (Leiden/Boston: Brill); Schreiber, J.Ph. (1992), 'L'immigration juive en Belgique: du Moyen Age à nos jours', in: Morelli, A. (ed.), *Histoire des étrangers et de l'immigration en Belgique. De la préhistoire à nos jours* (Brussels: EVO), 207-232; Michman, D. (2003), 'Problematic National Iden-

tity, Outsiders and Persecution: Impact of the Gentile Population's Attitude in Belgium on the Fate of the Jews in 1940-1944'. In: Bankier, D., I. Gutman (eds.), *Nazi Europe and the Final Solution* (Jerusalem: Yad Vashem), 455-468; Michman, D. (ed.) (2000), *Belgium and the Holocaust. Jews, Belgians, Germans* (Jerusalem: Yad Vashem), 43-114; Benbassa, E. (1999), *The Jews of France: a history from Antiquity to the Present* (Princeton, NJ: Princeton University Press); Birnbaum, P. (1994), 'Between social and political assimilation: remarks on the history of the Jews in France'. In: P. Birnbaum, I. Katznelson, eds., *Paths of Emancipation. Jews, States, and Citizenship* (Princeton: Princeton University Press), 94-127; Caron, V. (1999), *Uneasy Asylum. France and the Jewish Refugee Crisis, 1933-1942* (Stanford, CA: Stanford University Press).

12 Browning, Ch.R. (2004), *The Origins of the Final Solution: the Evolution of Nazi Jewish Policy, September 1939-March 1942* (London: William Heinemann), 193-194; Michman, D. (2011), *The Emergence of Jewish Ghettos during the Holocaust* (Cambridge/Jerusalem: Cambridge University Press/Yad Vashem), 42-89.

13 Paxton, R.O. (2001, revised ed.), *Vichy France: Old guard and New Order, 1940-1944* (New York: Columbia University Press); Jackson, J. (2003), *France: The Dark Years, 1940-1944* (Oxford/New York: Oxford University Press); Baruch, M.O. (1996), *Le régime de Vichy* (Paris: La Découverte), German edition: *Das Vichy-Regime: Frankreich 1940-1944* (Stuttgart: Reclam, 2000).

14 Guillon, J.M. (1992), 'La philosophie politique de la Révolution Nationale', in: Azéma J.P., F. Bédarida (eds.), *Le régime de Vichy et les Français* (Paris: Fayard/Institut d'Histoire du Temps Présent), 167-183; Yagil, L. (1997), *'L'Homme nouveau' et la Révolution nationale de Vichy, 1940-1944* (Villeneuve-d'Ascq, Nord: Presses universitaires du Septentrion); Baruch, M.O. (1997), *Servir l'État Français. L'administration en France de 1940 à 1944* (Paris: Fayard), 76-81, 97-109, 127-136, 229-233; Jackson, *France: The Dark Years*, 139-165 (Corporatism on 149 and 161-162), 327-353. For a lucid analysis of the concept and practice of Corporatism in this context, see: Le Crom, J.P. (1995), *Syndicats nous voilà! Vichy et le corporatisme* (Paris: Ouvrières); Luyten, D. (1997), *Ideologie en praktijk van het corporatisme tijdens de Tweede Wereldoorlog in België* (Brussels: VUB Press); idem (2004), 'Het sociale en economische leven. Rantsoenering, arbeidsverhoudingen en productie voor de Duitsers', in: Van den Wijngaert, M. et al., *België tijdens de Tweede Wereldoorlog* (Antwerp: Standaard), 67-124, esp. 80-81, 93-94.

15 Hirschfeld, *Nazi Rule*, 132-153; De Jong, *Het Koninkrijk*, vol. 4, 753-762, 868-871; Romijn, *Burgemeesters*, 176-188, 225-232; Van Doorslaer, R. (ed.)

(2007), *Gewillig België. Overheid en Jodenvervolging tijdens de Tweede Wereld-oorlog* (Antwerp etc.: Manteau/Meulenhoff/SOMA), 287-402; French language ed.: *La Belgique docile. Les autorités belges et la persécution des Juifs en Belgique durant la Seconde Guerre mondiale* (Brussels: CEGES/Éditions Luc Pire, 2007), chapter 8. Marrus, M.R., R.O. Paxton (1983), *Vichy France and the Jews* (New York: Schocken), 75-119 (chapter 3); Andrieu, C. (ed.) (2000), in co-operation with S. Klarsfeld et al., *La persécution des Juifs de France 1940-1944 et le rétablissement de la légalité républicaine. Recueil des textes officiels 1940-1999* (Paris: La Documentation française/Mission d'étude sur la spoliation des Juifs de France. Président: Jean Mattéoli).

16 De Jong, *Het Koninkrijk*, vol. 4, 762-803; Snoek, J.M. (1969), *The Grey Book. A collection of protests against anti-Semitism and the persecution of Jews, issued by non-Roman Catholic churches and church leaders during Hitler's rule* (Assen: Van Gorcum), 120-125.

17 Sijes, B.A. (1954), *De Februari-staking, 25-26 februari 1941* (The Hague: Martinus Nijhoff; English summary 215-228), 61-62, 89-96, 104-109, 139-168, 173-176, 181, 187-188, 203, 213, 219, 225-227; Moore, B. (1997), *Victims and Survivors. The Nazi Persecution of the Jews in the Netherlands* (London: Arnold), 71-73; Roest, F., J. Scheren (1998), *Oorlog in de stad. Amsterdam 1939-1941* (Amsterdam: Van Gennep), 229-245, 285-333, 447-457; Michman, *The Emergence of Jewish Ghettos*, 94-101, 125-127.

18 Steinberg, M. (1999), *Un pays occupé et ses juifs. Belgique entre France et Pays-Bas* (Gerpinnes: Quorum), 85-89; Struye, P. (1945/2004), *L' évolution du sentiment public en Belgique sous l'occupation allemande*, in: *Documents pour servir l'histoire de l'Occupation en Belgique*, vol. 1 (Brussels: Éd. Lumière, 1945), p. 70, 109; new ed.: Struye, P., Guillaume Jacquemyns, *La Belgique sous l'Occupation allemand (1940-1944)* (Brussels: Complexe/CEGES, 2004).

19 Berlière, J.M., with L. Chabrun (2001), *Les policiers français sous l'Occupation, d'après les archives inédites de l'épuration* (Paris: Perrin), 220-224; Kasten, B. (1993), *'Gute Franzosen'. Die französische Polizei und die deutsche Besatzungsmacht im besetzten Frankreich 1940-1944* (Sigmaringen: Jan Thorbecke), 96-97; Peschanski, D. (2002), *La France des Camps. L'internement, 1938-1946* (Paris: Gallimard), 201-202; Bruttmann, T. (2006), *Au bureau des affaires juives. L'administration française et l'application de la législation antisémite (1940-1944)* (Paris: La Découverte).

20 Lages, W.P.F. (1941/1952), 'Gesamtbetrachtung über den Februarstreik 1941 in Amsterdam', NIOD, arch. coll. 248: Doc I-998: Lages, Willi Paul Franz, folder R. De Jong, *Het Koninkrijk*, vol. 5, 543, 613-616; Aalders, G. (2004), *Nazi*

Looting: The Plunder of Dutch Jewry during the Second World War (Oxford: Berg); Griffioen & Zeller, *Jodenvervolging*, 220, 332 (n. 437), 340, 564-565.

21 Romijn, *Burgemeesters*, 243-247; Meershoek, G. (1999), *Dienaren van het gezag. De Amsterdamse politie tijdens de bezetting* (Amsterdam: Van Gennep), 169-170, 215; Presser, J. (1988), *Ashes in the Wind. The Destruction of Dutch Jewry* (Detroit: Wayne State University Press), 69-70, 80-81, 97, 108, 144, 155, 322-323; Moore, *Victims*, 81-84, 89, 93-94; De Jong, *Het Koninkrijk*, vol. 5, 548-553, 558-560; Griffioen & Zeller, *Jodenvervolging*, 220, 223 (n. 243), 317 (n. 350).

22 Romijn, *Burgemeesters*, 240, 243, 446, 452 n. 56; Griffioen & Zeller, *Jodenvervolging*, p. 317 n. 348 on p. 789, p. 318 (n. 354-356), p. 324 (n. 392-395), p. 318-324. Van Doorslaer (ed.), *Gewillig België*, chapter 9; Vandepontseele, S. (2004), 'Le travail obligatoire des Juifs en Belgique et dans le nord de la France'. In: Schreiber J.Ph. & R.Van Doorslaer (eds.), *Les Curateurs du ghetto: l'Association des Juifs en Belgique sous l'occupation nazie* (Brussels: Labor),189-231; Fraser, D. (2009), *The Fragility of Law. Constitutional Patriotism and the Jews of Belgium, 1940-1945* (New York: Routledge); Meinen, I. (2009), *Die Shoah in Belgien* (Darmstadt: Wissenschaftliche Buchgesellschaft), 30-33.

23 Joly, L. (2006), *Vichy dans la 'Solution finale'. Histoire du commissariat général aux Questions juives (1941-1944)* (Paris: Bernard Grasset); Marrus/Paxton, *Vichy France and the Jews*; Klarsfeld, S. (1983), *Vichy-Auschwitz: le rôle de Vichy dans la 'solution finale de la question juive' en France*, vol. 1: *1942* (Paris: Fayard); Baruch, *Servir l'État français*.

24 De Jong, *Het Koninkrijk*, vol. 5, 543, 614; Van der Boom, B. (2003), *'We leven nog.' De stemming in bezet Nederland* (Amsterdam: Boom), 109-113, 122; Griffioen & Zeller, *Jodenvervolging*, 332-333, 564-565.

25 Burrin, *France under the Germans*, 22-23, 31, 175-176, 178; Marrus/Paxton, *Vichy France*, 16, 209; Laborie, P. (1990), *L'Opinion française sous Vichy* (Paris: Seuil/l'Univers historique); idem (1992), 'The Jewish Statutes in Vichy France and Public Opinion'. In: *Yad Vashem Studies* 22 (Jerusalem: Yad Vashem), 89-114, esp. 94; Jackson, *France*, 272-274, 370-374; Alary, É., et al. (2006), *Les Français au quotidien, 1939-1949* (Paris: Perrin). Struye, *L'évolution du sentiment public en Belgique*, 70, 109; Schreiber, J.Ph. (2003), 'Belgium and the Jews under Nazi rule: beyond the myths', in: Bankier/Gutman (eds.), *Nazi Europe and the Final Solution*, 469-488, esp. 479-480.

26 Michman, D. (2003), 'Problematic National Identity, Outsiders and Persecution: Impact of the Gentile Population's Attitude in Belgium on the Fate of the Jews in 1940-1944'. In: Bankier & Gutman (eds.), *Nazi Europe and the Fi-*

nal Solution, 455-468; Schreiber, 'Belgium and the Jews under Nazi rule: Beyond the myths'. Poznanski, R. (2001), *Jews in France during World War II* (Hanover, NH, and London/Washington DC: Brandeis University Press/ USHMM), 242-244; Laborie, *L'Opinion française sous Vichy*, chapter 4: 'Printemps 1942-hiver 1942-1943: les ruptures et la lassitude', 262-281; Sweets, J.F. (2003), 'Jews and Non-Jews in France during the Second World War', in: Bankier & Gutman (eds.), *Nazi Europe and the Final Solution*, 361-373, esp. 370-371.

27 For an international comparison of imposed Jewish organizations, see: Michman, D. (2003), 'Jewish Headships under Nazi Rule: The Evolution and Implementation of an Administrative Concept', in: Michman, D., *Holocaust Historiography: A Jewish Perspective. Conceptualizations, Terminology, Approaches and Fundamental Issues* (Portland/London: Vallentine Mitchell), 159-175. For the AJB in Belgium, see: Schreiber, J.Ph., R. van Doorslaer (eds.) (2004), *Les Curateurs du ghetto: l'Association des Juifs en Belgique sous l'occupation nazie* (Brussels: Labor); Meinen, *Die Shoah*, 59-82. For the UGIF in France, see: Adler, J. (1987), *The Jews of Paris and the Final Solution: Communal Response and Internal Conflicts, 1940-1944* (New York/Oxford: Oxford University Press), and Cohen, R.I. (1987), *The Burden of Conscience: French Jewish leadership during the Holocaust* (Bloomington/Indianapolis: Indiana University Press). For the Amsterdam Jewish Council in the Netherlands, see: De Jong, *Het Koninkrijk*, vol. 4, chapter 18; vol. 5, chapters 6 & 12; vol. 6, chapters 1 & 4; vol. 7, chapter 2; Presser, *Ashes*, chapter 4, esp. the extensive paragraph on p. 238-277; Moore, *Victims*, chapter 6; Lindwer, W., in cooperation with Houwink ten Cate, J. (1995), *Het fatale dilemma. De Joodsche Raad voor Amsterdam, 1941-1943* (The Hague: SDU).

28 Express letter from Adolf Eichmann to the German Foreign Office (Auswärtiges Amt), June 22, 1942, *Akten zur deutschen auswärtigen Politik 1918-1945*, Series E: 1941-1945, vol. 3 (1974), 43. Cf. Klarsfeld, S., M. Steinberg (eds.) (1980), *Die Endlösung der Judenfrage in Belgien: Dokumente* (New York/Paris: Beate Klarsfeld Foundation/CDJC), 28-29. Cesarani, D. (2004), *Eichmann. His life and crimes* (London: William Heinemann), 139-140.

29 Kasten, B., *'Gute Franzosen'*, 21, 28; idem (2000), 'Zwischen Pragmatismus und exzessiver Gewalt. Die Gestapo in Frankreich 1940-1944', in: Paul, G., K.M. Mallmann (eds.), *Die Gestapo im Zweiten Weltkrieg. ,Heimatfront' und besetztes Europa* (Darmstadt: Wissenschaftliche Buchgesellschaft), 362-382, esp. 364, 368-370; Umbreit, *Militärbefehlshaber*, 111-112; Marrus/Paxton, *Vichy France*, 241 n. 91.

30 'Aktenvermerk' by Herbert-Martin Hagen, July 4, 1942, CDJC doc. XXVI-40,

in: Klarsfeld, S. (ed.) (1979-1980), *Recueil de* [2000] *documents des dossiers des autorités allemandes concernant la persécution de la population juive en France (1940-1944)* (New York/Paris: The Beate Klarsfeld Foundation; 11 vols.; henceforth: *Recueil*), vol. 4, 1000-1009; Klarsfeld, S. (1989), *Vichy-Auschwitz. Die Zusammenarbeit der deutschen und französischen Behörden bei der 'Endlösung der Judenfrage' in Frankreich* (translated from the French by Ahlrich Meyer. Nördlingen: Greno), 90-93, 393-397; Kasten, *'Gute Franzosen'*, 26-28, 69-73, 97-99; Froment, P. (1994), *René Bousquet* (Paris: Stock), 190-197; Berlière/Chabrun, *Les policiers français*, 32-34, 227 n. 2, 229.

31 Steinberg, M. (2004), *La Persécution des Juifs en Belgique (1940-1945)* (Brussels: Complexe), 193 n. 4, 304 n. 78; Verhoeyen, É. (1994), *La Belgique occupée. De l'an 40 à la Libération* (Brussels: De Boeck-Wesmael), 534; Meinen, *Die Shoah*, 44-50, 87, 109, 147-148, 166-170.

32 Fijnaut, C., G. Meershoek, J. Smeets, R. van der Wal (2004), 'The Impact of the Occupation on the Dutch police', in: Fijnaut, C. (ed.), *The Impact of World War II on Policing in North-West Europe* (Leuven: Leuven University Press), 91-132, 100-101; De Jong, *Het Koninkrijk*, vol. 5, 467-470; Romijn, *Burgemeesters*, 455.

33 Meershoek, G., *Dienaren*, 152ff., 172-189, 248; idem (1992), 'De Amsterdamse hoofdcommissaris en de deportatie van de joden', in: Barnouw, N.D.J. et al. (eds.), *Oorlogsdocumentatie '40-'45: Derde Jaarboek van het Rijksinstituut voor Oorlogsdocumentatie* (Zutphen: Walburg Pers), 9-43, esp. 24 and 40 n. 76; idem (1998), 'The Amsterdam Police and the Persecution of the Jews', in: Berenbaum, M. and A.J. Peck (eds.), *The Holocaust and History: The Known, the Unknown, the Disputed, and the Reexamined* (Bloomington: Indiana University Press in association with the United States Holocaust Memorial Museum), 284-300.

34 Klarsfeld (1989), *Vichy-Auschwitz*, chapters 4, 5, 6; Baruch, *Servir l'État*, 101-102, 226; Berlière/Chabrun, *Les policiers français*, 226-229, 236-241, 247; Kasten, *'Gute Franzosen'*, 98-100, 168; Bruttmann, *Au bureau des affaires juives*, passim; Cohen, A. (1993), *Persécutions et sauvetages: Juifs et Français sous l'Occupation et sous Vichy* (Paris: Cerf), 269-282; Marrus/Paxton, *Vichy France*, 250-279; Seibel, W. (2010), *Macht und Moral. Die 'Endlösung der Judenfrage' in Frankreich, 1940-1944* (Konstanz: Konstanz University Press), esp. chapters 6 and 7. For the American political and diplomatic pressure on the French government in August and September 1942, see: Ministère des Affaires Étrangers (MAE)-C 140, cited in Klarsfeld (1989), *Vichy-Auschwitz*, 156; Otto Abetz to Auswärtiges Amt, August 31, 1942, doc. AA 3762 in Yad Vashem Archives (YVA), Jerusalem, text in Klarsfeld (1989), *Vichy-Ausch-*

witz, 447. Telegram, September 16, 1942, by French ambassador Henri Haye in Washington D.C. to the French Ministry of Foreign Affairs, reprinted in: Klarsfeld (1983), *Vichy-Auschwitz. Le rôle de Vichy*, vol. 1: *1942* (original French edition), 438-439 (not included in the 1989 German edition). Cohen, A., *Persécutions*, 299; Wyman, D.S. (1984), *The Abandonment of the Jews. America and the Holocaust 1941-1945* (New York: Pantheon Books), 36-37.

35 Steinberg, M. (1984), *L'Étoile et le Fusil*, vol. 2: *1942: les cent jours de la déportation des Juifs de Belgique* (Brussels: Vie Ouvrière), 180, 193-193 n. 25-27; idem (2004), *La Persécution*, 233-250; Meinen, *Die Shoah*, 42-43, 84.

36 De Jong, *Het Koninkrijk*, vol. 6, 339-340; Presser, *Ashes*, 143-145, 155-156, 158-159, 391-392; Romijn, *Burgemeesters*, 442; Moore, B. (2010), *Survivors. Jewish self-help and rescue in Nazi-occupied Western Europe* (Oxford: Oxford University Press), 214; idem, *Victims*, 152; Van der Boom , B., (2012), *'Wij weten niets van hun lot'. Gewone Nederlanders en de Holocaust* (Amsterdam: Boom), 394-401.

37 For Belgium, see: Steinberg, M., *L'Étoile et le Fusil*, vol. 2, 177-181, 195-199, 207; idem, *La Persécution*, 233-250, 267-280; Saerens, L. (2005), *Étrangers dans la cité. Anvers et ses Juifs (1880-1944)* (Brussels: Labor), 698-724 (chapter 10); Van Doorslaer, et al., *Gewillig België*, 568-576; Meinen, *Die Shoah*, 41-48, 83-84. For the Netherlands, see: Presser, *Ashes*, 140, 149, 158-163; Moore, *Victims*, 92-95; Meershoek, *Dienaren*, 234-247.

38 For Belgium, see: Steinberg, M., *L'Étoile et le Fusil*, vol. 2, 114-116, 216-218; vol. 3: *La traque des Juifs, 1942-1944* (2 sub-volumes, Brussels: Vie Ouvrière, 1986), sub-vol. 1, 40-46, 75-81; Steinberg, L. (1973), *Le Comité de Défense des Juifs en Belgique, 1942-1944* (Brussels: Centre national des hautes études juives/Éditions de l'Université de Bruxelles); Michman, ed., *Belgium and the Holocaust*, 347-455; Meinen, *Die Shoah*, 92-95, 113-147 (chapter 4), 182-185. For France, see: Adler, *The Jews of Paris*, chapter 9; Cohen, A., *Persécutions et sauvetages*, 383-386, 445-448, 482-488; Zuccotti, S. (1993), *The Holocaust, the French, and the Jews* (New York: BasicBooks), chapter 12; Poznanski, R., *Jews in France*, chapter 11; Belot, R. (1998), *Aux frontières de la liberté. Vichy-Madrid-Alger-Londres. S'évader de France sous l'Occupation* (Paris: Fayard); Yagil, L. (2005), *Chrétiens et Juifs sous Vichy (1940-1944). Sauvetage et désobéissance civile* (Paris: Cerf), esp. the Second Part with regional studies (per *département*), 121ff.

39 'Abschrift, Geheim, Niederschrift über die Besprechung bei dem Herrn Reichskommissar am 16.10.1942 betr. Sortierung der Juden', NIOD, Arch. HSSPF, BdS, IV B 4, file 183f, p. 1 (see also microfilm 311). 'Rüstungs-Inspektion Niederlande' to the Generalkommissar für das Sicherheitswesen,

Rauter, December 2, 1942, NIOD, Arch. HSSPF, IV B 4, file 172b. The report by IV B 4-The Hague 'Entwicklung der jüdischen Rückstellungsgruppen in den Niederlanden (Stand 20. März 1943)', NIOD, Arch. HSSPF, VI, BdS, file 181a, see also English translation in: L.Ph. Polak, L. van Weezel, eds. (1979), *Documents of the persecution of the Dutch Jewry 1940-1945* (Amsterdam: Jewish Historical Museum/Athenaeum – Polak & Van Gennep), 124-129. Statement by Wilhelm Harster during his trial in Munich, February 9, 1966, cited in: Kempner, R.M.W. (1968), *Edith Stein und Anne Frank. Zwei von Hunderttausend. Die Enthüllungen über die NS-Verbrechen in Holland vor dem Schwurgericht in München. Die Ermordung der 'nichtarischen' Mönche und Nonnen* (Freiburg im Breisgau: Herder), 156. Cf. De Jong, *Het Koninkrijk*, vol. 6, 227-228, 270-274, 316-317; Presser, *Ashes*, 166-167 (demoralization). Houwink ten Cate, J.Th.M. (1989), '"Het jongere deel". Demografische en sociale kenmerken van het jodendom in Nederland tijdens de vervolging'. In: *Oorlogsdocumentatie '40-'45. Jaarboek van het Rijksinstituut voor Oorlogsdocumentatie 1989* (Amsterdam/Zutphen: De Walburg Pers), 9-66, esp. 16, 20-23, 27-35; idem (1999), 'Mangelnde Solidarität gegenüber Juden in den besetzten niederländischen Gebieten?'. In: W. Benz, J. Wetzel, eds., *Solidarität und Hilfe für Juden während der NS-Zeit: Regionalstudien 3; Dänemark, Niederlande, Spanien, Portugal, Ungarn, Albanien, Weissrussland* (Berlin: Metropol), 87-133, esp. 109-111; Lindwer, *Het fatale dilemma*, 28-29, 53-54.

40 For Amsterdam, see: Meershoek, 'Amsterdamse hoofdcommissaris', 35 and note 130 on p. 43; idem, *Dienaren*, 249, 258, 267-272, 288; idem, 'The Amsterdam Police'. For Rotterdam, see: Van der Pauw, J.L. (2006), *Rotterdam in de Tweede Wereldoorlog* (Amsterdam/Meppel: Boom), 338-339, 361-363; Van Riet, F. (2008), *Handhaven onder de Nieuwe Orde. De politieke geschiedenis van de Rotterdamse politie tijdens de Tweede Wereldoorlog* (Zaltbommel: Aprilis), chapter 9. For the exception of The Hague, see: Van der Boom, B.E. (1995), *Den Haag in de Tweede Wereldoorlog* (The Hague: Lakerveld), 91-92, 100-107. For the city of Utrecht, see: Vernooij, A. (1985), *Grenzen aan gehoorzaamheid: houding en gedrag van de Utrechtse politie tijdens de Duitse bezetting* (Utrecht: Trezoor), 66-69; Regenhardt, J.W. (2002), *In de schaduw van de Dom. Overleven in de stad van de NSB* (Amsterdam: Uitg. Bas Lubberhuizen), 116-117. For the cities of Groningen and Utrecht, and other towns, see: Croes, M., Tammes, P. (2004), *'Gif laten wij niet voortbestaan'. Een onderzoek naar de overlevingskansen van joden in de Nederlandse gemeenten, 1940-1945* (Amsterdam: Aksant; English summary 593-608), 192-193, 253-256, 471-477. For the towns of Enschede and Hengelo in the eastern Twente re-

gion: Schenkel, M.J. (2003), *De Twentse paradox. De lotgevallen van de joodse bevolking van Hengelo en Enschede tijdens de Tweede Wereldoorlog* (Zutphen: Walburg Pers), 80-82. On these special, pro-German units under direct German control, which operated independently from the regular Dutch police, *in general*, see: De Jong, *Het Koninkrijk*, vol. 6, 226, 244-246, 250; Hirschfeld, *Nazi Rule*, 175-176; Moore, *Victims*, 206-209; Romijn, *Burgemeesters*, 455; Houwink ten Cate, 'Mangelnde Solidarität gegenüber Juden in den besetzten niederländischen Gebieten?', 101 n. 81, 102 n. 83, 105; idem (2002), 'Der Judenmord als NS-Staatskriminalität unter massenhafter einheimischer Beteiligung. Forschungsstand und Ausblick auf Grund des Einzelbeispiels Niederlande', in: Houwink ten Cate, J., A. Kenkmann (eds.), *Deutsche und holländische Polizei in den besetzten niederländischen Gebieten. Dokumentation einer Arbeitstagung* (Münster: Villa ten Hompel), 118-130, esp. 126-128; Meershoek, G. (2002), 'Motive der niederländische Beihilfe an der Deportation der Juden: Pflichtbewusstsein oder Habgier und Opportunismus?', in: *Deutsche und holländische Polizei*, 104-117, esp. 105 n. 5.

41 Presser, *Ashes*, 169-173; De Jong, *Het Koninkrijk*, vol. 6, 237-241, 343; Van der Boom, *Den Haag*, 91-92; Van der Poel, S. (2004), *Joodse Stadjers. De joodse gemeenschap in de stad Groningen, 1796-1945* (Assen: Koninklijke Van Gorcum), 141-143; Croes/Tammes, 'Gif', 341.

42 Telex from Helmut Knochen to Adolf Eichmann, September 25, 1942, CDJC doc. XXVc-177, in: *Recueil*, vol. 6, 1550-1551. Klarsfeld (1989), *Vichy-Auschwitz*, 179-183.

43 Note ('Aufzeichnung') by Karl-Theodor Zeitschel (German Embassy, Paris), September 16, 1942, CDJC doc. DLXVI-10, in: *Recueil*, vol. 5, 1484-1486; cf. report by Heinz Röthke (Judenreferat, Paris), September 1, 1942, *ibid.*, 1384-1385. Griffioen/Zeller, 'Anti-Jewish Policy', 455.

44 Klarsfeld/Steinberg (eds.), *Die Endlösung*, 60; Steinberg, M., *L'Étoile et le Fusil*, vol. 2; idem, *La Persécution*, 292-299; Buysse, L., R. van Doorslaer et al. (2001), *De Bezittingen van de slachtoffers van de Jodenvervolging in België. Spoliatie, Rechtsherstel. Eindverslag van de Studiecommissie betreffende het lot van de bezittingen van de leden van de joodse gemeenschap in België, geplunderd of achtergelaten tijdens de oorlog 1940-1945* (Brussels: Office of the Prime Minister), 39, 44-51; French language ed.: *Les Biens des Victimes des Persécutions anti-juives en Belgique. Spoliation, Rétablissement des droits* (see also: http://www.combuysse.fgov.be); Meinen, *Die Shoah*, 92-95, 172-175, 182-184; Griffioen/Zeller, *Jodenvervolging*, 422-424, 445, 620-621, 667, 1009.

45 For Belgium: Selleslagh, F. (ed.) (1993), *De verplichte tewerkstelling in Duits-*

land – 1942-1945 – Le Travail obligatoire en Allemagne. Acta van het symposium gehouden te Brussel op 6 en 7 oktober 1992 / Actes de symposium tenu à Bruxelles les 6 et 7 octobre 1992 (Brussels: Centre de Recherche et d'Études historiques de la deuxième Guerre mondiale); Colignon, A. (1993), 'La résistance et l'aid aux réfractaires du travail obligatoire'. In: Selleslagh, ed., *De verplichte tewerkstelling – Le Travail obligatoire*, 121-132; Van Doorslaer (ed.), *Gewillig België*, 604-605, 609. For France: Pierre Laborie (1980), *Résistants, vichyssois et autres* (Parijs: CNRS), 285; Cohen, A., *Persécutions et sauvetages*, 362; Jackson, *France*, 503. For the Netherlands: Bouman, P.J., Sijes, B.A. (1950), *De April-Mei Stakingen van 1943* (The Hague: Martinus Nijhoff; English summary 437-456), 187-188; Sijes, B.A. (1966), *De Arbeidsinzet: de gedwongen arbeid van Nederlanders in Duitsland 1940-1945* (The Hague: Martinus Nijhoff); Warmbrunn, W. (1972), *The Dutch under German Occupation 1940-1945* (Oxford: Oxford University Press), 74-75, 113-118; De Jong, *Het Koninkrijk*, vol. 7, 799-806, 844-861; Van der Boom, '*Wij weten niets van hun lot*', 405.

46 Presser, *Ashes*, 184-192; De Jong, *Het Koninkrijk*, vol. 6, 318-319, 326-329; Van der Boom, *Den Haag*, 165-166; Meershoek, *Dienaren*, 266; Moore, *Victims*, 100; Houwink ten Cate, 'Mangelnde Solidarität', 106 n. 107.

47 Militärverwaltungschef (General Reeder), 'Tätigkeitsbericht', no. 22, December 31, 1942, CDJC doc. CDXCVI-6, cited in M. Steinberg, *L'Étoile et le Fusil*, vol. 2, 229 n. 82; idem, *La Persécution*, 298 n. 108. Saerens, L. (2007), *De Jodenjagers van de Vlaamse SS. Gewone Vlamingen?* (Tielt: Lannoo). For the AJB-homes: Steinberg, M., *L'Étoile et le Fusil*, vol. 3.1, 156-160, 167-171, 218-219; Brachfeld, S. (1992), *Ils n'ont pas eu ces gosses. L'histoire de plus de 500 enfants 'fichés à la Gestapo' et placés pendant l'occupation allemande dans les homes de l'Association des Juifs en Belgique (AJB)* (Hezliya: IRJB); idem (2000), 'Jewish orphanages in Belgium under the German occupation', in: Michman (ed.), *Belgium and the Holocaust*, 419-431; Massange, C. (2004), 'La politique sociale', in: Schreiber/Van Doorslaer (eds.), *Les Curateurs*, 277-316; Meinen, *Die Shoah*, 79-80.

48 Minutes of the Amsterdam Jewish Council, Central Committee, 86th meeting, March 26, 1943, p. 1, NIOD, Arch. Coll. 182: Joodsche Raad voor Amsterdam, 1c. Idem, meeting of Thursday April 8, 1943 ('Auffangslager'). Koker, D. (1993), *Dagboek, geschreven in Vught* (Diary, written in the Vught concentration camp, 1943. Amsterdam: G.A. van Oorschot, 3rd ed.), 101 (April 17, 1943). Presser, *Ashes*, 465-466; De Jong, *Het Koninkrijk*, vol. 6, 330-332; vol. 8, 712-725, esp. 721 n. 1. Meeuwenoord, M. (2011), *Mensen, macht en mentaliteiten achter prikkeldraad. Een historisch-sociologische*

studie van concentratiekamp Vught (1943-1944). Doctoral dissertation, University of Amsterdam, 401-402 (Eng. summary).

49 Schelvis, J. (2007), *Sobibor: A History of a Nazi Death Camp* (Oxford/Washington DC: Berg Publishers/USHMM). De Jong, *Het Koninkrijk*, vol. 7, chapter 2; vol. 8, 865-883.

50 Kempner, *Edith Stein und Anne Frank*, 31-38, 78, 88-92, 151-157. Houwink ten Cate, J. (1998), 'Der Befehlshaber der Sipo und des SD in den besetzten niederländischen Gebieten und die Deportation der Juden 1942-1943', in: W. Benz, J. Houwink ten Cate, G. Otto (eds.), *Die Bürokratie der Okkupation. Strukturen der Herrschaft und Verwaltung im besetzten Europa* (Berlin: Metropol), 197-222. Meyer, A. (2010), *Das Wissen um Auschwitz. Täter und Opfer der 'Endlösung' in Westeuropa* (Paderborn etc.: Ferdinand Schöningh), 57-70. Ritz, Ch. (2012), *Schreibtischtäter vor Gericht. Das Verfahren vor dem Münchner Landgericht wegen der Deportation der niederländischen Juden (1959–1967)*. Griffioen & Zeller, *Jodenvervolging*, 226-227, 432-441, 767 n. 265.

51 Umbreit, *Militärbefehlshaber*, 62-63; Paxton, *Vichy France*, 280-288; Marrus/Paxton, *Vichy France and the Jews*, 302-303.

52 Klarsfeld (1989), *Vichy-Auschwitz*, 199, 202-205, 224, 228-232, 238-239, 256-257, 270; Klarsfeld, S. (1992), 'The Influence of the War on the Final Solution in France'. In: A. Cohen, Y. Cochavi, Y. Gelber, eds., *The Shoah and the War* (New York etc.: Peter Lang), 271-281; Marrus/Paxton, *Vichy France*, 323-329; Zuccotti, *Holocaust*, 177-178; Seibel, *Macht und Moral*, chapters 8 and 11.

53 Carpi, D. (1994), *Between Mussolini and Hitler: The Jews and the Italian Authorities in France and Tunisia* (Hanover, NH: University Press of New England), 125-126; Zuccotti, S. (1987), *The Italians and the Holocaust: persecution, rescue and survival* (New York: Basic Books), 82-100; Klarsfeld (1989), *Vichy-Auschwitz*, 194-199, 206-207, 213-215, 218-228, 233-234, 247-249, 256-257, 260-261, 267-268, 276-283; Marrus/Paxton, *Vichy France and the Jews*, 315-321; Seibel, *Macht und Moral*, chapter 9.

54 Report by Heinz Röthke, March 6, 1943, CDJC doc. XXVc-214, in: *Recueil*, vol. 7, p. 1950-1951. Report by Röthke, March 27, 1943, CDJC doc. XLVI-chem.VI, in: *Recueil*, vol. 8, p. 2073-2076. Klarsfeld (1989), *Vichy-Auschwitz*, 208-209, 216-217, 223-224, 264-266.

55 Report by Röthke, July 21, 1943, doc. Oberg 13; VIII Z, in: Klarsfeld (1989), *Vichy-Auschwitz*, 241, 545-547. Report by Röthke, August 15, 1943, CDJC doc. xxvii-36, in *ibid.*, 551-553; Aktenvermerk, Oberg; Hagen, August 25, 1943, CDJC doc. xxvii-39, in *ibid.*, 556. Cf. Marrus/Paxton, *Vichy France*, 329-331; Felstiner, M. (1986), 'Alois Brunner: Eichmann's Best Tool'. In: *Si-*

mon Wiesenthal Center Annual vol. 3, 1-46; idem (1987), 'Commandant of Drancy: Alois Brunner and the Jews of France', *Holocaust and Genocide Studies* vol. 2, no. 1, 21-47; Hafner, G.M., Schapira, E. (2000), *Die Akte Alois Brunner: Warum einer der größten Naziverbrecher noch immer auf freiem Fuß ist* (Frankfurt am Main: Campus), 106-135; Cesarani, *Eichmann*, 128, 147-148; Kitson, S. (2002), 'From Enthusiasm to Disenchantment'. In: *Contemporary European History*, vol. 11, no. 3 (Cambridge University Press), 371-390, esp. 382. Seibel, *Macht und Moral*, chapter 12.

56 For France: Klarsfeld (1989), *Vichy-Auschwitz*, 284-290, 295-296, 308-309; Poznanski, *Jews in France*, chapters 10-11; Zuccotti, *Holocaust*, chapters 11-15. For Belgium: Steinberg, L., *Le Comité*; Steinberg, M., *L'Étoile et le Fusil*, vol. 3.1; Saerens, L. (2004), 'Die Hilfe für Juden in Belgien'. In: W. Benz, J. Wetzel, eds., *Solidarität und Hilfe für Juden während der NS-Zeit. Regionalstudien 4: Slowakei, Bulgarien, Serbien, Kroatien mit Bosnien und Herzegowina, Belgien, Italien* (Berlin: Metropol), 193-280, esp. 277-278; Saerens, L. (2007), *De Jodenjagers van de Vlaamse SS. Gewone Vlamingen?* (Tielt: Lannoo); Meinen, *Die Shoah*, 154-155, 182-185. For the Independence Front in Belgium, see: Mark van den Wijngaert et al., *België in de Tweede Wereldoorlog*, 221-222, 231-237.

57 Klarsfeld (1989), *Vichy-Auschwitz*, 320, 324-328.

58 Steinberg, M., *L'Étoile et le Fusil*, vol. 2, 156-164; vol. 3.2, 222-226; Van Doorslaer (ed.), *Gewillig België*, 565, 632-633.

59 Griffioen & Zeller, *Jodenvervolging*, 496-499 (France), 532-535 (Belgium), 560-564 (The Netherlands), 579-580. For France, see also: Klarsfeld (1989), *Vichy-Auschwitz*; Berlière/Chabrun, *Les policiers français*; Kasten, 'Gute Franzosen'. For Belgium, see also: Steinberg, M., *La Persécution*, 132, 234, 279, 298; Meinen, *Die Shoah*, 170-172, 222 n. 98. For the Netherlands, see also: Meershoek, *Dienaren*; Houwink ten Cate, J. (1994), 'Alfons Zündler en de bewaking van het gevangenkamp aan de Plantage Middenlaan 24 te Amsterdam – volgens de geschreven bronnen'; unpublished report (Amsterdam: Netherlands Institute for War Documentation, also submitted to Yad Vashem, Jerusalem), statistical appendix; Houwink ten Cate, 'Mangelnde Solidarität?', 101 n. 81, 102 n. 83, p. 105; idem, 'Der Judenmord als NS-Staatskriminalität', esp. 126-128; Meershoek, 'Motive der niederländische Beihilfe an der Deportation der Juden: Pflichtbewusstsein oder Habgier und Opportunismus?', esp. 105 n. 5.

Areal view of camp Vught, 1944.

The Holocaust in the Netherlands: new research of camp Vught
by Marieke Meeuwenoord

Camp Vught was built in 1942 by order of the Higher SS and Police Leader in the Netherlands Hanns Albin Rauter. It was the only concentration camp in the Netherlands that fell under direct command of the Business Administration Main Office in Berlin, which made it an official SS concentration camp modelled after the so-called *Dachauer Modell*. The *Dachauer Modell* was developed at the beginning of the 1930s by Theodor Eicke who was commander of Dachau at that time. His *Modell* created coerced societies where under the pretext of disciplining by order and labour prisoners were subjected to terror and violence to be dehumanized and depersonalized.

Besides a *Schutzhaftlager* for male and female prisoners and hostages, camp Vught was also built as a transit camp for Jews. The camp was divided into several sub camps. It consisted of a Jewish camp, a *Schutzhaftlager* for male prisoners, a women's camp, a camp for students who were taken hostage, a police transit camp and a sub camp of the Security Service.

When the first groups of prisoners arrived in January 1943 the campsite was far from finished. As a result, more than 300 people died during those first months from diseases and lack of food. In the course of 1943 circumstances improved and the number of deaths decreased, except for the last three months, in the summer of 1944, when approximately 350 members of resistance groups were executed in the woods near the camp. When camp Vught was evacuated in September 1944 about 32,000 people had been incarcerated there and about 750 people had died there.

1. The historiography of camp Vught

The first reports about camp Vught were written as soon as the camp was evacuated in September 1944. Within three years some twenty former prisoners felt compelled to tell and publish their story. This shows that there was no collective silence or repression of memory in the first years after the war. Quite the opposite. The number of eyewitness accounts both of Vught and of other camps was so substantial that the audience soon became saturated. At the end of the 1940s the focus was on rebuilding society and therefore there was no attention for individual suffering. Also, the majority of the population did not want to be confronted with the war-period because of feelings of moral guilt towards the Jews.

From the end of the 1940s onwards eyewitness accounts stopped being published, but the history of the war continued to be written, for many years, by survivors. *Onderdrukking en Verzet. Nederland in oorlogstijd*, translated as *Oppression and Resistance. The Netherlands in wartime,* was the first official publication and was seen as a closure of the war-period.[1] Part of this study was a long contribution by Holocaust survivor Abel Herzberg who wrote *Kroniek der Jodenvervolging* translated as *Chronicles of the persecution of the Jews* which was both nationally and internationally one of the first studies about the Holocaust.[2]

The main theme of *Oppression and Resistance* was that the majority of the Dutch population had successfully resisted the German occupier and that they had not been infected by the propaganda of the National-Socialists. This way the authors deliberately created a national memory with a focus on 'good' and 'bad', the resistance and the suffering of the population, without regard to the experiences of specific groups, such as Jewish citizens. For decades this focus was dominant in Dutch historiography.

In 1950 the historian Jacques Presser was asked to write a book about the history of the persecution of the Jews in the Netherlands. Fifteen years later this resulted in the publication of *The destruction of the Dutch Jews*. His study was mainly based on so-called ego documents, a collective term for autobiographies, diaries, memoirs and personal letters. For his account of camp Vught Presser had mainly used two ego documents. The first was a report from Arthur Lehmann, a camp inmate who had been the Camp Elder. The second was a diary kept by David Koker. He was a 21-year-old student and former pupil of Presser. Koker had a privileged position in the camp, and as a result Presser wrote the history of the camp mainly through the eyes of prisoners who held certain positions, the so-called *Funktionshäftlingen*. This led to a limited focus on regular camp life. The SS-guards and camp leaders were hardly mentioned in his book. He noted only: 'We know some of these people generally well, in many camp reports we see them act as wicked men, brutal, incompetent, cruel, rude.'[3]

A more extensive discussion of the history of the camp was published in 1978 as part of Loe de Jong's magnum opus *Het Koninkrijk der Nederlanden in de Tweede Wereldoorlog,* translated: *The Kingdom of the Netherlands during the Second World War.* His fifty pages on camp Vught were the most detailed account of the camp for more than thirty years.[4] De Jong paid much attention to the organization of the camp, the living conditions, the work commandos and the numbers of the different groups of prisoners in the camp.

De Jong, in line with Presser, made frequent use of ego documents and used a specific selection. His focus on the camp history was mainly on the male *Schutzhaft* prisoners. Jewish and female prisoners were hardly mentioned. He wrote even less about the SS-guards and camp leaders. He was the first author to give short biographical descriptions of the camp commanders, but spent only two paragraphs on male and female guards.

Several Dutch historians have written about Vught since the end of the 1970s. They mainly focused on facts about the organization of the camp, the number of prisoners and the conditions of life. They followed in Presser's and De Jong's tradition. All in all, the historiography of camp Vught mainly focused on the history of the male prisoners in the *Schutzhaftlager* and the *Funktionshäftlingen* in the Jewish camp. Historians did not differentiate between the experiences of the various groups of prisoners and paid little attention to the camp commanders, the German and Dutch SS and the *Aufseherinnen*.

2. Main topics of German historiography

After De Jong, historical research of the concentration camps in the Netherlands came to a halt, whereas in Germany, since the mid-1980s, the Nazi concentration camps have become the subject of sustained historical research. The main questions of my PhD thesis were thus extracted from German historiography. For instance, in order to study the background and behaviour of the camp commanders, I used the work of sociologist Karin Orth.[5] Several German historians wrote about the behaviour and use of power and violence by female guards as compared to male SS guards. I cannot discuss all my findings in this article and will therefore concentrate on the following three questions.

First of all, during the last decades German historiography paid more and more attention to the fact that the purpose and function of the camps, the organization, the living conditions and the constitution of the prisoners changed over time. An important study on this topic is *The order of terror by* sociologist Wolfgang Sofsky.[6] He studied the power system in the camps. He stressed that it was not enough to look solely at the behaviour of the SS but that their behaviour had to be put into perspective. Sofsky wrote that the social reality of the camp is quite different from the aims and objectives of the top organizational echelon of the SS. Rather, its everyday life was shaped by dependencies and antagonisms among beneficiaries, personnel, auxiliaries and victims.[7] Therefore, one of my main questions was: what were the objectives of the German occupier with regard to camp Vught and in what way did these objectives influence the behaviour of the camp commander and SS guards and, subsequently, the lives of the prisoners.

Another important issue which is related to Sofsky's study derives from the work of Falk Pingel titled *Häftlinge unter SS-Herrschaft*, translated as *Prisoners under SS-Dominion*. Over the years the behaviour of the guards in camp Vught was only discussed in terms of terror. A thorough reading of eyewitness accounts and the study of judicial records shows that the interaction of the guards and prisoners had more dimensions. Falk Pingel wrote in 1978 that he believed that the system of coercion that was being used in the concentration camps could not be simply enforced from above. The guards would have to take into account the attitude and reactions of the prisoners. Pingel wondered in what way the reactions of the prisoners differed from the expectations of the guards and to what extent the SS had to be lenient from time to time to keep order.[8] It was my aim to answer these same questions with regard to camp Vught.

In line with Pingel, historians like Hermann Kaienburg and Olaf Mussmann researched in what way differences in social, economic, religious and ideological background of the prisoners, as well as the grounds on which they were arrested and their expectations about their future, influenced the social stratification and hierarchy within and between the various groups of prisoners. Since camp Vught consisted of several sub camps I considered this an important question.

To answer these questions I based my research on ego documents, such as diaries, contemporary letters, early accounts of prisoners and memoirs of a later date. In the first years after the war, the RIOD, now NIOD Institute for War, Holocaust and genocide Studies, collected over 250 reports from prisoners. Together with the seven diaries that were preserved, hundreds of clandestine letters and almost fifty published accounts, I had a vast amount of sources at my disposal. For information about the camp leaders and male and female guards I went to the National Archives in The Hague, where the judicial files are kept for all men and women prosecuted for war-related crimes. I studied more than 120 files of both German and Dutch, male and female guarding personnel. I also studied the SS personnel files in the *Bundes Archiv* in Berlin.

3. Comparing camp Vught with concentration camps in Germany

It is important to stress that although camp Vught was broadly the same as the SS camps in Germany, it was not a direct copy. For one, this is shown by the number of deaths in regard to the other camps. During the twenty months of its existence, 2 per cent of the population died in Vught, whereas in Dachau and Mauthausen the death rate was between 15 and 25 per cent. This indicates that camp Vught differed substantially from concentration camps in Germany.

The specific character of camp Vught becomes apparent in the objectives of the main SS and Police leader Rauter. He wanted Vught to be an orderly led camp where conditions of life for the prisoners were relatively good. In German camps, the commanders and guards had, as Sofsky wrote, 'absolute power' but the three camp commanders that successively led camp Vught were instructed personally by Rauter to limit the use of violence.[9] The Dutch population heard that the conditions of life in Police Transit Camp Amersfoort were extremely bad. This had had a negative effect on the reputation of the German occupier and Rauter wanted to improve that reputation. Because of Rauter's instructions the use of violence was indeed less excessive and deadly than in other concentration camps. SS guards used other order measures such as allowing the prisoners to cook extra food, wear more clothes and to practice their religion. They also arranged afternoons with sports and film screenings and offered the opportunity for the prisoners to organize musical performances and cabaret in the evening. This way conditions of life were less destructive.

Because of German personnel shortages, Dutch male and female guards were used to watch over the prisoners. Because the guards and prisoners had the same nationality and spoke the same language the hierarchy between them was less pronounced. Only a few Dutch guards were as violent as their German SS colleagues. Most of the Dutch guards followed orders without being extremely violent. A substantial number of guards were even willing to help prisoners by smuggling letters or messages and letting them work slowly, though sometimes in exchange for money or other things. This also led to the fact that conditions of life were less disastrous in camp Vught.

It was typical of camp Vught that the different groups of prisoners were incarcerated in separate sub camps, some of them divided by barbed wire. The three main sub camps were the male *Schutzhaftlager*, the Jewish camp and the camp for female prisoners. The sub camps were distinguished by the power of the SS, the hierarchic structure and the differences in social stratification that was created by the prisoners. I will focus mainly on my findings of the Jewish sub camps in comparison to the other sub camps.

4. The Jewish sub camp in Vught

The Jewish sub camp opened in January 1943 with the arrival of 450 Jewish men, women and children from Amsterdam. Two and half months later the number had increased tenfold to over 4,500. And in May 1943 more than 8,000 Jews were incarcerated in camp Vught. After that, the size of outgoing transports – the length of the trains – exceeded the size of incoming transports, and the number of interned Jews decreased. In November 1943, only 500 Jews were left and they remained in Vught until June 1944.

The German occupier had led the Jews in Vught to believe they could stay there for the duration of the war. They would have to work, but would not be deported. In order to maintain this myth the Jews were allowed to keep their baggage, were called detainees instead of prisoners and did not have to wear a prisoners' uniform. Furthermore, the Jews were in charge of the organization of the Jewish sub camp. The camp commander appointed a camp elder, and two Jewish helpers and several hundreds of prisoners were put to work in daily camp life. The SS leaders and guards hardly showed themselves in the Jewish sub camp. This was a deliberate strategy to avoid alarm.

But soon it became apparent that the Germans would not keep their promises. The first outgoing transport left at the end of January, so only two weeks after the opening of the camp. Because it concerned a small group of elderly people, it seemed consistent with the plan to make Vught a labour camp. But the number of transports increased. In May 1943 it became clear that camp Vught would not be a detention centre but a transit camp and that it was most likely that nobody would remain.

Despite the fact that the direct display of power by the SS in the Jewish camp was relatively limited, the SS dominated the Jews more than the other groups of prisoners. The threat of being deported had a solid grip on the Jewish prisoners. In futile hope to avoid deportation the detainees obediently followed the orders of fellow prisoners and the SS and they hardly dared to offer resistance. The SS maintained a strict rule and was less lenient in comparison to other sub camps. Although SS surveillance was much more prominent in the non-Jewish sub camps, these prisoners did dare to offer resistance and created a greater degree of latitude with respect to the SS.

The fact that the Jewish prisoners were responsible for organizing daily life influenced the hierarchy within the Jewish sub camp. The *Funktionshäftlingen* had superior power over the 'normal' prisoners which led to a gap between the two groups. More than in other sub camps, the Jewish *Funktionshäftlingen* related differently to the SS and their fellow prisoners. They concentrated on obeying the orders of the SS, not only to protect their privileged position but also because they believed it to be in the best interest of all prisoners. The SS had threatened to take over power if the *Funktionshäftlingen* did not maintain order, and they figured that if the SS would take over control, things would be worse.

The social stratification within the Jewish camp was dominated by the fact that Jews were incarcerated with families and friends. Although, there were thousands of Jewish prisoners differing in age, religious beliefs, social background and nationality, family ties and former friendships remained the starting point of social relations, even though men and women were incarcerated separately. This way the diversity of backgrounds was not manifest in a strict social hierarchy. The most evident social gap was between German and Dutch prisoners since the German

Jews were more often appointed in important positions. The Dutch prisoners doubted their loyalty and often referred to their 'German way' of obeying orders, which meant strict and at top speed.[10] Other than that, there was no distinct social hierarchy or stratification and families formed the pivot of social relations.

The men's *Schutzhaftlager* was the counterpart of the Jewish sub camp. In addition to the four categories of prisoners distinguished by the SS, namely political prisoners, so-called 'anti-socials', Jehovah's Witnesses and hostages, the *Schutzhaft* prisoners made distinctions between various political beliefs, social economic background and nationality. This resulted in a complex social stratification. Noteworthy for camp Vught was that the social economic background of the *Schutzhaft* prisoners still played an important role. Men who in 'normal' society had been part of the higher social classes were spared by the *Funktionshäftlingen* and were put in less exhausting working groups. The prisoners also had an eye for the fact that hostages deserved a better treatment because they were incarcerated through no fault of their own.

The last topic I want to discuss is the way the non-Jewish prisoners perceived their Jewish fellow-prisoners. In clandestine letters the male and female *Schutzhaft* prisoners expressed their dismay about the dramatic scenes when the Jews were getting ready for deportation. Terms like 'heart rendering' and 'heartbreaking' were often used. However, references to the fact that the Jewish citizens were locked up in camps for no good reason, being entirely at the mercy of the German Nazis and their cruel and murderous plans, were hardly made. This silence is even more notable because quite a few non-Jewish prisoners wrote in explicit terms about the fate of the Jews. One prisoner wrote about a transport with mainly children and their parents: 'to know that they all run, hobble, walk and the children frolic to their planned extermination in Auschwitz or Mauthausen'.[11]

Partly, the lack of protest against the treatment of the Jews was due to latent anti-Semitism. It was also affected by the different ways the two groups, Jews and non-Jews, were treated by camp leaders and the German occupier. In the first months after the opening of the camp the Jewish prisoners had been privileged. The non-Jews were exhausted by their imprisonment in camp Amersfoort, had hardly any luggage or food and had to work hard to finish building the camp, while the Jewish detainees did not have to work during these first months, because the factories and workshops were not ready yet. This led to jealous feelings towards the Jews who in the words of one prisoner 'did not have anything to do all day except walking around in their warm clothes and fur coats'.[12]

After May 1943 the situation reversed. Many of the privileges of the Jews were taken away and they constantly feared deportation. Because of the impeding, deportation Jewish prisoners worked hard and did not dare to offer resistance. The reports of the non-Jewish prisoners show that they were annoyed by the helplessness and the servility of the Jews towards the SS. The internment of the Jews did strengthen the idea that they had to have done something wrong to deserve such a treatment. These feelings were mixed with relief that the non-Jews were not the main subject of hatred by the German SS. So in the end, the way the non-Jewish prisoners perceived their Jewish fellow-prisoners was ambivalent. On the one hand they felt for them and pitied them when they saw them getting ready for deportation; but on the other they seemed indifferent to their fate.

To sum up: because of the objectives of Rauter and the German occupier with regard to camp Vught and the use of Dutch guarding personnel next to the German SS the conditions of life in the camp were relatively good. Therefore, it was possible to uphold certain social structures, moral values and parts of Dutch culture. It was typical of camp Vught that there were several groups of prisoners incarcerated in different sub camps. My PhD thesis showed that although the prisoners were brought together behind one barbed wire fence and were led by one central leadership, camp Vught was not a unity. It is therefore actually impossible to speak of one camp and the history of camp Vught. Camp Vught was an assembly of sub camps. The prisoners were subjected to several forms of power and within each sub camp a specific hierarchy and social stratification was formed.

Notes

1 Bolhuis; J.J. van, e.a. (eds.), s.a. [1950-1954]. *Onderdrukking en verzet. Nederland in oorlogstijd*, vol. 1-4. Arnhem/Amsterdam: Van Loghum Slaterus/J.M. Meulenhoff.

2 Herzberg, A. (1956) *Kroniek der Jodenvervolging*. Arnhem/Amsterdam: Van Loghum Slaterus/J.M. Meulenhoff.

3 Presser, J. (1965) *Ondergang. De vervolging en verdelging van het Nederlandse Jodendom 1940-1945*, vol. 2. Den Haag: Martinus Nijhoff, 391.

4 Jong, L. de (1978) *Het Koninkrijk der Nederlanden in de Tweede Wereldoorlog*, vol 8 part 2, *Gevangenen en gedeporteerden*. Den Haag: Staatsuitgeverij, 606-662.

5 Orth, K. (2000) *Die Konzentrationslager-SS. Sozialstrukturelle Analysen und biographischen Studien*. Göttingen: Wallstein Verlag.

6 Sofsky, W. (1993) *Die Ordnung des Terrors: Das Konzentrationslager*. Frankfurt am Main: Fischer Verlag.

7 Ibid., 18-19.

8 Pingel, F. (1978) *Häftlinge unter SS-Herrschaft. Widerstand, Selbstbehauptung und Vernichtung im Konzentrationslager*. Hamburg: Hoffmann und Campe, 10.

9 Sofsky, *Ordnung*, 22.

10 Assou-Polak, Verklaring, Nederlands Instituut voor Oorlogsdocumentatie (NIOD), Vught, Konzentrationslager Herzogenbusch (250g), inv.nr. 528 p. 4; Koker, D., 2006 (1st edn 1977). *Dagboek*. Amsterdam: Uitgeverij G.A. van Oorschot, 25, 46-47.

11 Van Wijk, 'Bedrijfskroniek', NIOD, 250g, inv.nr. 775, 16.

12 Alderding, Verklaring, NIOD, 250g, inv.nr. 521, 6.

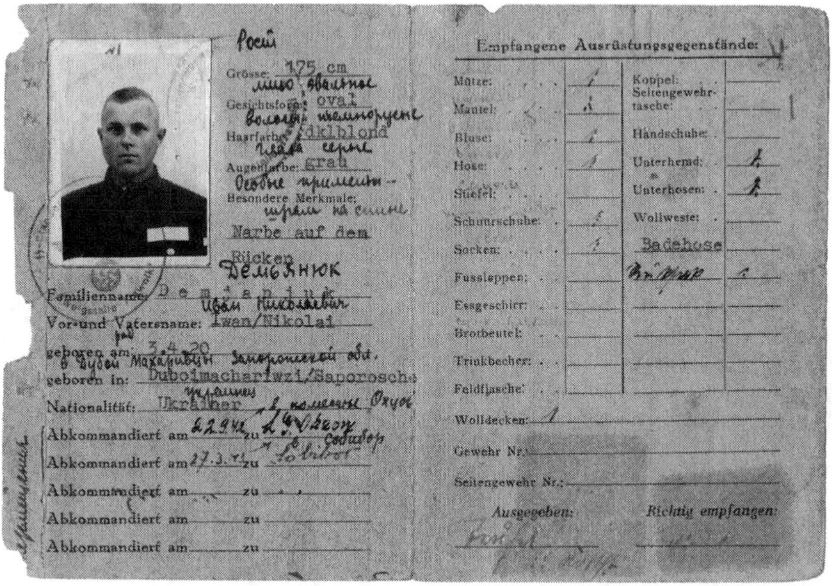
Grösse: 175 cm
Gesichtsform: oval
Haarfarbe: dklblond
Augenfarbe: grau
Besondere Merkmale: Narbe auf dem Rücken
Familienname: Demjanjuk
Vor- und Vatersname: Iwan/Nikolai
geboren am: 3.4.20
geboren in: Duboimachariwzi/Saporosche
Nationalität: Ukrainer
Abkommandiert am 22.9.42 zu L.G. Okszow
Abkommandiert am 27.3.43 zu Sobibor
Abkommandiert am zu
Abkommandiert am zu
Abkommandiert am zu

Empfangene Ausrüstungsgegenstände:

Mütze: 1
Mantel: 1
Bluse: 1
Hose: 1
Stiefel:
Schnürschuhe: 1
Socken: 1
Fusslappen:
Essgeschirr:
Brotbeutel:
Trinkbecher:
Feldflasche:
Koppel:
Seitengewehrtasche:
Handschuhe:
Unterhemd: 1
Unterhosen: 1
Wollweste:
Badehose
Wolldecken: 1
Gewehr Nr.:
Seitengewehr Nr.:
Ausgegeben:
Richtig empfangen:

Identity card of Demjanjuk.

Looking back on the German Holocaust trials and the last Nazi trial in Munich against John Demjanjuk
by Johannes Houwink ten Cate

Introduction

This essay firstly focusses on how the post-war German legal system dealt with the Holocaust. My second question concerns how I – as one of the former advisors of the Dutch co-plaintiffs and of the (expert-) witnesses in this case – should look back upon the last German trial which dealt with the Holocaust, that is to say the trial against John/Ivan Demjanjuk (1920-2012) in Munich (2009-2011).[1]

1. The Nazis – three groups of perpetrators

In order to evaluate the efficiency of the post-war German legal system in dealing with Holocaust perpetrators, some knowledge of the perpetration of the Holocaust is needed. During this specific genocide, which was not unique but was most certainly unprecedented,[2] human beings defined as Jews were murdered in roughly three different ways: in the ghettos of Eastern Europe 800,000 people died; approximately 1.3 million Jews were murdered in mobile operations, that is to say they were shot in open air; and the majority of the victims – up to three million of them – most of them Polish – were murdered in non-mobile facilities.

The most famous of these non-mobile murder operations naturally is Auschwitz-Birkenau, where the Jews of Greece and Hungary were murdered. The Polish Jewry was murdered in three other (extermination) facilities: in Treblinka, Belzec and in Sobibor.[3] As other genocides, the

Holocaust was essentially a group phenomenon. It took place because ordinary men decided to participate; and these ordinary men did not act on their own but as a group. In the Holocaust three different groups or types of men participated: there were – firstly – the thousands of civil servants, who paved the way for mass murder.[4] These thousands of civil servants did not murder anyone themselves. They did not leave their desks. Very few of them were specialists, in the sense that they were primarily engaged in Jewish Affairs. Usually they managed Jewish Affairs on a part-time basis, as a minor part of their regular work load.[5] Secondly, there were the occasional murderers (such as the men from the German Order Police) who participated in the mobile murder operations;[6] and thirdly there were the professional murderers in the non-mobile operations. My estimate of that last group, the professional murderers in the non-mobile operations, is that it would not be higher than say 2,000.[7]

2. The perpetrators that were or were not brought to German Justice

According to calculations made by the Dutch scholar Dick de Mildt, up to 1992 '755 persons stood trial [in Western Germany-JHtC] for their war-time involvement in the systematic persecution and killing of Jews'.[8] In the period 1945 to 1952 five trials took place with altogether twelve desk perpetrators as defendants; from 1953 to 1959 no trials with desk perpetrators took place. In the period 1967 to 1987, the years in which the percentage of cases involving Jewish dead rose from 29 per cent to 76 per cent of all cases relating to the Nazi period, 14 trials took place with 27 defendants who had been desk perpetrators.[9] This means that the civil servants who part-time managed Jewish Affairs were not punished. The most important legal problem involved was that the responsibility of a desk murderer for a murder that takes place far away is by no means easy to prove. You need some kind of smoking gun, in the form of a direct order. On the other hand, some of the desk murderers had been in charge of mobile murder operations in the field. Both groups overlapped, and these men were not brought to trial either.[10]

There was a general lack of political will to punish desk murderers/civil servants. The most blatant example of this was the case of the judges who had handed down death sentences on Jews and Gentiles during the Third Reich. Now, obviously desk murderers were to be found here who had themselves ordered murders. These judges were not even forced to resign; nor did they lose their pensions, for that matter. It was not until 1989 that German federal judges described this as the scandal it undoubtedly was. [11] Evidently, legal systems do not automatically purify themselves. This is sometimes a result of the involvement of legal experts in atrocities as civil servants. In my view, this obvious failure of the German legal system illustrates the fact that it takes a lot of political pressure before a legal system is able to deal with new types of defendants; the natural reflex of a legal system under pressure is to repeat its traditional successes, and to go for the more traditional types of defendants.

German society as a whole repressed the involvement of the ordinary German military in the atrocities that had taken place in the East until more than thirty years after the war. Historians themselves were in many ways responsible for this: the first book on the involvement of the German military in the implementation of the Holocaust was not published until 1978. [12]

As far as the 2,000 professional murderers in the non-mobile murder operations were concerned, the German legal system did make a real effort, starting in the beginning of the 1960s and reaching its peak in the middle of the 1960s and during the 1970s.

Now, you may think that many of these professional murderers who had worked in the extermination facilities had escaped to South America. Although some of them did (Eichmann, Mengele, Stangl), most of them did not, for an organization of former SS-members in South America has never existed. These hardened murderers were living in Germany; they were usually arrested in their home towns, living ordinary lives. Some of them even held minor jobs in the German civil service. [13]

In these matters the German legal system had to make obvious decisions as to how to deal with these 2,000 professional murderers involved in the extermination facilities.

Three decisions were made. Firstly, only the Germans who had worked in these facilities were to be brought to German Justice; their Eastern European assistants were not indicted. Most of these Eastern Europeans were not living in Germany anyway. Many of them had not survived the war; others had been tried and shot by the Soviet authorities. A tiny minority of these Eastern Europeans fooled the American authorities and emigrated to the United States. The decision to let the Eastern European assistants be, limited the number of potential defendants to around 400 German officers and men.

The second decision made was that the extermination facility was neither seen as a society in its own right, nor as a more or less autonomous factory of death, but as a low level of the German hierarchy. The practical result was that even the higher ranking German men in an extermination facility, for example the extermination facility of Sobibor (170,000 Jewish victims), were not indicted as co-perpetrators but rather more typically as accomplices in mass murder. The most important co-perpetrators (Hitler, Himmler, Göring, Heydrich, Globocnik and Wirth), after all, were very much dead.

The third and final decision was to make a distinction between the enthusiastic German professional murderers on the one hand and the not so enthusiastic or even unwilling professional German murderers on the other, on the basis of eyewitness testimonies provided by the Jewish survivors of these extermination facilities; these were the so-called 'Work Jews' who had escaped, but still had vivid memories of their German masters.[14]

Within these limitations the German system proved to be highly efficient. The indictments were prepared by a specialized federal bureau. The American Office for Special Investigations of the Justice Department was more or less modelled on this German predecessor. The huge advantage of this was that Public Prosecutors at the district level did not waste much time in preparing the indictments. Just how efficient the system was becomes apparent in the case of the German masters of the Sobibor extermination facility.

A total of 77 German lower ranking officers and men had worked in

Sobibor in total. They directed the murder of 170,000 mostly Polish Jews in the period May 1942 to October 1943.

Of these 77 men, 25 had died before the end of the War. Two of them were pronounced legally dead in 1951 and 1954 respectively. That left the authorities with 50 possible defendants. One of them died in 1948 and three lived in Eastern Germany, behind the Iron Curtain. This reduced the group of 77 to 46.

Of these 46 men 23 men could not be found, because they had fled from Germany or – more probable – because they too had gone missing during the war. The remaining 23, however, were all brought to justice; six men were acquitted, five of them because they had pleaded a specific form of duress.[15] I will return to this fascinating topic later on.

It is fair to say that the favourite defendant of the German system was by no means the former judge, nor was he the former general, nor was he the former military officer. The German legal system went for the German professional mass murderers responsible for the death of the majority of the Jewish victims in the non-mobile murder operations, in the factories of death that is, and within this last group the individual guilt of the defendants was as precisely defined as possible.

3. The trial against Demjanjuk

John Demjanjuk died on 17 March 2012, and therefore there will not be an appeal stage at the federal level. This means that I am at long last at liberty to say how I feel about this particular trial. In my review of this last Sobibor trial, and perhaps the last Nazi trial, I will focus on the written verdict – a lengthy document of 220 pages – that was made available by the Munich District judges in October 2011.

In this verdict the judges explained who Demjanjuk was, where he worked, and why they were sending this man to prison for five years as an accomplice in mass murder in the Sobibor extermination facility in 1943.[16]

The publication of the written verdict enables us to review for what

Demjanjuk was indicted, to discuss the basic issues of this trial and how the judges decided upon these issues. And to look back on the role that expert witnesses played during these proceedings.

4. The indictment

John Demjanjuk was born in 1920, in the Soviet Union, in Ukraine.[17] He emigrated to the United States after the Second World War. When applying for emigration, Demjanjuk wrote that during the war he worked as a truck driver in Sobibor, a Polish village.[18]

Demjanjuk stood trial in Israel in the 1980s. He was suspected of being the man nicknamed 'Ivan the Terrible' in Treblinka. This man supposedly operated the engines that gassed the victims. He thus was responsible for the deaths of hundreds of thousands of human beings.

Given the death penalty by Jerusalem District judges in 1988, Demjanjuk appealed, maintaining that he was a victim of mistaken identity. Demjanjuk won the appeal. And in 1993 the Israeli government sent him back to the United States.[19]

A new German investigation started in June 2008. The preparation of the indictment took two prosecutors four months. Demjanjuk was extradited to Germany in May 2009. His trial began in November of that year.

The backbone of the trial was the indictment written by the Munich prosecutor Dr. Hans-Joachim Lutz. Dr. Lutz maintained that Demjanjuk worked as a simple guard, holding the lowest rank, in another extermination facility, Sobibor, in the period March to September 1943.

In Sobibor, from May 1942 until October 1943, an estimated 170,000 Jews were murdered. 19 per cent of the Sobibor victims were deported from the occupied Dutch territories; 23 per cent of the Dutch Jews were murdered there.[20]

This trial was a novelty in two respects. It marked one of the first times in German legal history that a non-German national had to stand trial for the murder of non-German nationals during the Third Reich; a murder that took place outside of Germany proper – namely, in Poland.[21] Formally this part of Poland was not annexed by the Third Reich but formed a separate political entity, the so-called *General Government*.

This trial, with the 'no-frills' indictment of Demjanjuk as being an accomplice in murder, was exceptionally novel in the sense that the indictment described the mass murder in Sobibor as a single process. Implicating all those present in Sobibor in the extermination.

For the first time, a non-German low-ranking guard was indicted even though there is no proof of him having perpetrated a specific offense, apart from his alleged being an accomplice in murder.[22]

According to the indictment all men working there herded the Jews to their death.[23] A grand total of 160 men worked in Sobibor; about twenty to thirty German men, and 100 to 150 Eastern European men trained in the town of Trawniki.

In his indictment the prosecutor wrote that Demjanjuk was a German civil servant who was trained in the village of Trawniki near Lublin, also in eastern Poland. Just like some 5,000 other Eastern Europeans who were trained there. This status as a civil servant meant that German judges had jurisdiction.

The 5,000 men from Trawniki served – as Dr. Peter Black has named them – as 'the foot soldiers' of the Holocaust. [24]

In Germany, these Trawniki men were not brought to trial up until two years ago. In the Soviet Union, however, numerous trials of Trawniki men have taken place.

One of these defendants, a Trawniki man by the name of Ignat Danilchenko, stated in the Soviet Union in 1949 that he saw Demjanjuk herding Jews to their deaths in Sobibor.[25] This is the only statement by an eyewitness that Demjanjuk was seen in Sobibor.[26]

The indictment relied on Dr. Peter Black – formerly with the Office for Special Investigations in the U.S. Justice Department and now with the United States Holocaust Memorial Museum in Washington.

Peter Black maintained that, while many other Trawniki men left their ranks without permission of their superiors, Demjanjuk evidently stayed in Sobibor because he wanted to. He therefore had the intention to work there; in other words, he was a willing foot soldier.[27]

In a direct reaction to Demjanjuk's death sentence in Jerusalem in 1988, a German expert, Helge Grabitz, the Senior Public Prosecutor in Hamburg, had previously written that the Trawniki men erroneously believed that their refusal of orders would lead to their death at the hands of their German masters.[28]

Dr. Black wrote that Demjanjuk was a willing foot soldier, whereas Prosecutor Grabitz had previously written that Demjanjuk as a Trawniki man acted out of fear. This meant that these Trawniki men were not responsible in a legal sense of the word. And if they were not responsible in a legal sense, then there was no point in bringing them to trial.

Now that no more than two other Trawniki men were alive and living in Germany,[29] the indictment of Demjanjuk dealt in detail with the extermination in Sobibor of 28,000 persons.

During the summer of 1943, when Demjanjuk allegedly worked there, some 45,000 Jews were murdered in Sobibor,[30] most of whom originated from the occupied Dutch territories. Only the transports from the Netherlands have been recorded in transport lists and only the personal identities of the victims from the Netherlands are known, as well as some of the identities of the victims in a transport from the Polish town of Izbica.[31]

None of the handful of Jewish survivors of Sobibor still alive today retain memories of Demjanjuk.[32] The German authorities wrote they did not need such witnesses because the historical documentation would suffice to address the essential issues. Before I discuss these issues, I would first like to make some general remarks on trials such as these.

5. Domestic and international trials

Formally this trial undoubtedly was a domestic trial. The jurisdiction of the Munich District Judges was based on the view that as a Trawniki man working in Sobibor, Demjanjuk was a German civil servant. Furthermore, the indictment – him having been an accomplice in murder – was a traditional domestic indictment.

But this trial was an international trial as well, in the sense that Demjanjuk stood trial as a non-German national, who was being held accountable for the murder of non-Germans.

The heart of this matter is that – as international trials tend to do – the Demjanjuk trial was a high profile trial dealing with atrocious deeds that took place outside of Germany more than half a century ago, and that these atrocities were perpetrated in a society which is very different from the society in which the trial took place.

In international trials the documentary evidence is relatively scarce. This means that the prosecutor needs much time to prepare the indictment. Preparing the indictment may take many months, as it did this time. In preparing the indictment the prosecutor of foreign atrocities is often dependent upon eyewitnesses whose reliability is not easy to assess. In this respect the prosecutor's position is not unlike that of an experienced reporter.

And if these eyewitnesses are lacking – as they were during the Demjanjuk trial with the exception of the statement by Danilchenko – the prosecutor will need expert witnesses; that is to say witnesses who are not eyewitnesses, but who provide legal testimony in the form of professional opinions.

At the end of the day, the prosecutor has no other option than to rely upon the reputation of his eyewitnesses and his expert witnesses. In other words, in trials like these the position of the prosecutor is weaker than in run-of-the-mill domestic trials, while at the same time the stakes are higher, because the preparation of the indictment has taken so much time. Furthermore, the trial itself is high profile.

In trials such as these the positions of the defendant and his defence also are relatively weak. The media despise the defendant. And the options of the defence are limited. The defence only has two viable options: to deny that the defendant was present and to deny that the defendant was responsible.

During this trial the strategy of the defence was the following. Demjanjuk was to remain silent about Sobibor. He did not utter a single word about his role in this extermination facility. His defence has maintained that the historical documentation placing Demjanjuk in Sobibor was forged. The defence maintained that Demjanjuk was never there; or, if he was, he was in no way involved in the gassings; or, if he was involved in them, he stayed there because he knew or had heard that deserting Trawniki men were put to death by their German masters.[33]

This last line of defence was somewhat theoretical, mainly because Demjanjuk did not speak about his role in Sobibor. And it is not so easy to maintain that a defendant acted out of fear, if that defendant is not willing to admit that he acted at all.[34]

To put this in other words, the defence might have opted for another strategy, and that strategy might have been to have the defendant admit that he worked in Sobibor, but that he did this because his German masters scared him to death, and that he was therefore not responsible. But this was not the way the defence wanted to go.

The judges in hybrid trials like these – trials that are domestic as well as international – have to re-interpret their role as well, as much as the Prosecutors, the expert witnesses and the defence are re-interpreting their roles.

It is the task of the judges to describe the atrocities and comment on the responsibility of the defendant. And in trials such as these there is always a group dimension, but the legal process deals with individuals. If members of a group sit in the dock of the defendant, they are sitting there as individuals. Judges, however, are not used to deal with the group dimension of mass atrocities; this, obviously, is a result of the fact that (European) prosecutors usually make do without indictments in which the group dimension is of the essence.

6. Basic issues in the proceedings

There were four basic issues in the proceedings:

1) Did the defendant work in Sobibor?
According to the verdict, Demjanjuk worked in Sobibor. The authentici-

ty of Demjanjuk's Trawniki identity papers was discussed at length. The German expert witness Dr. Anton Dallmayer found these papers to be authentic.[35]

The list of Trawniki men sent to Sobibor in March 1943 – a list that included the name of Demjanjuk – was authentic as well.[36] The judges remarked this also on the basis of the testimony of the forensic expert Larry F. Stewart, who researched the typewriting and type of paper of twelve Trawniki identity papers.[37]

That the list of Trawniki men sent to Sobibor was real in the sense that these men were actually sent to Sobibor was apparent from the testimony of Danilchenko. In 1949, in the Soviet Union, Danilchenko identified Demjanjuk as one of the other guards who had herded the Jews to their deaths.[38] The judges wrote that this statement by Danilchenko was accurate,[39] as was apparent from other statements made by other Trawniki men in the Soviet Union.[40] Generally speaking, the judges found these statements by Trawniki men in the Soviet Union to be accurate descriptions of their work and of their knowledge of the fate of the deported Jews.[41]

2) If the defendant was in Sobibor, were Jews murdered there during that time?

According to the verdict, there were Jews murdered in Sobibor while the defendant worked there. Most of the Jews murdered in Sobibor while Demjanjuk was working there were deported to Sobibor from Westerbork, a transit facility in the occupied Dutch territories. Their personal data (name and date and place of birth) were typed on transport lists, and these transport lists were published by Drs. Jules Schelvis in 2001.[42]

I have testified as a witness, and not as an expert witness, on the authenticity of the Dutch transport lists, for the defence successfully doubted my impartiality. Previously I had written a report for Prosecutor Lutz, in which I explained how these transport lists were drafted by the Jewish staff in the transit facility of Westerbork, and how the final transport lists had been typed and by whom. The prosecutor invited another Dutch expert witness, Dr. Regina Grüter. She testified that these lists were authentic as well, and the judges used my previous statement as an endorsement of the statements made by Dr. Grüter.[43]

Dr. Grüter added something highly important, which was that she proved that a number of the victims deported from the Netherlands had German nationality. This matter had bearing on the problem of jurisdiction.[44]

3) Was there a division of labour in Sobibor?
The verdict stresses that there was no division of labour. Two survivors of Sobibor, Thomas Blatt and Philip Bialowitz, have testified that there was no division of labour there, and that all of the men trained in Trawniki herded Jews to the building in which they were gassed.
During their trials in the Soviet Union many former Trawniki men admitted the same. The noted German historian Dr. Dieter Pohl testified as an expert witness on the operation of the Sobibor extermination facility and the role played by the Trawniki men there. On the basis of all of these statements the judges wrote that as a guard Demjanjuk was an accomplice to the destruction of the deportees, for Sobibor had no other purpose.[45]

It may be true that the judges did not know the exact whereabouts of Demjanjuk in Sobibor during the murders, but they wrote that he was 'eingebunden in das Gesamtgefüge der Bewachungsorganisation' [he was a permanent part of the overall guard organization].[46]

As in Treblinka and Belzec, in Sobibor each and every guard was an accomplice as they formed parts of a death machine.[47]

4) Was it possible for the men trained in Trawniki to flee from Sobibor? And if they did, and were apprehended, were they then murdered by their German masters?
The debate on the possibilities of leaving Sobibor, with or without the permission of the German superiors, and on the punishment of arrested deserters, was a long one. The judges maintained that many Trawniki

men did in fact flee.[48] They wrote that it was possible to flee from Sobibor, as two other Trawniki men fled from Sobibor on July 1, 1943.[49]

Dr. Dieter Pohl testified as an expert witness. He stated that those men from Trawniki who left their duties without permission of their superiors and were arrested were indeed put to death if they were caught with a firearm. Dr. Pohl claimed that deserters that left unarmed were not shot but merely punished.

The judges, who read a number of documents on the desertions of Trawniki men aloud, maintained that Demjanjuk was aware of this, and that Demjanjuk was morally obliged to make the effort of trying to flee (without a firearm) but that he obviously did not.[50]

Therefore, in all of the four decisive issues in this trial the expert witnesses played an important role. This trial is an example of the important role expert witnesses can play in trials in which there are no eyewitnesses.

But the experts are not the only ones in trials such as these who are redefining their roles: so are the prosecutors, who are dependent upon the reputation of the expert witnesses, and so are the judges, who have to tell historical tales. The judges have to solve novel and under-researched historical problems – such as the matter how Trawniki men were treated by their superiors after they were arrested as deserters with or without a firearm. This means that the traditional division of labour between the realm of the law and the realm of history writing is a thing of the past; it may have become a historical phenomenon in itself.

In holding the view that all men working in extermination facilities as Belzec, Treblinka and Sobibor were accomplices in mass murder, the Munich judges stated that the German legal system should not have ignored the non-German Trawniki foot soldiers of the Final Solution for such a long time. This statement is tantamount to stating that the German legal system of the past has handled the – admittedly perennial –[51] problem of the accomplices in too restricted a way; a way that – very obviously – has not stood the test of time.

7. Some personal observations on this trial

Now that Demjanjuk is dead, we will never know how the Federal German judges would have evaluated the verdict of the Munich District Court, but I would like to make some personal observations, and these observations suggest that this verdict was debatable in three respects.

The prime witness, Ignat Danilchenko, was dead and therefore not available for interrogation; his statement was regarded by the judges as trustworthy nevertheless.

The statements made by other Trawniki men were also regarded as trustworthy, although these statements as the ones made by Danilchenko were products of the Soviet legal system. This legal system is infamous, inter alia because so many defendants admitted to atrocities never performed by them. The fact that many Trawniki-trained men described their guilt in using the very same words points to the fact that these statements may have been what the defence maintained they were: simple fabrications by the Soviet authorities.

The Munich District Judges should perhaps have refrained from discussing very technical historical matters, such as the fate of arrested Trawniki men who had fled from their duties with or without a firearm. Sometimes, the pursuit of history is indeed technical; in my view that is all the more true when discussing the niceties of the legal system of the SS and the German Police.

Notes

1 Paragraphs IV-VIII of this contribution were almost entirely previously published by me under the title: 'Looking back on the Demjanuk Trial in Munich', in: *Jewish Political Studies Review*, 1 March 2012, no. 116, 11 pp. That part was read by my friends Dr. Wichert ten Have, Mr. Manuel Bloch and Prof.mr. Harmen van der Wilt. I thank them for their kind help.

2 The best general work on the Holocaust is: R. Hilberg, *The Destruction of the European Jews* (New York and London: Holmes & Meier, 1985), 3 vols. For the word 'unprecedented', see ibidem, vol.1, 8.

3 For data on Jewish deaths by cause, see Hilberg, *The Destruction*, vol. 3, 1219.

4 See Hilberg, *The Destruction*, vol, 1, 55-56.

5 Hilberg, *The Destruction*, vol. 1, 62.

6 For this group, see Christopher R. Browning, *Ordinary Men. Reserve Police Battalion 101 and the Final Solution in Poland* (New York: HarperCollins, 1992), passim.

7 The number of men working in the extermination camps Sobibor, Treblinka and Belzec was small (see below). In by far the largest murderous camp of Auschwitz-Birkenau only 1.5 per cent of the SS men present worked for the Political Department which supervised the mass destruction of human lives. Piper has calculated that this group counted no more than one hundred men; Franciszek Piper, *Auschwitz 1940-1945. Studien zur Geschichte des Konzentrations- und Vernichtungslagers Auschwitz*, vol. 1 (Oswiecim: State Museum Auschwitz-Birkenau 1999), 195, 219.

8 De Mildt, D., *In the Name of the People: Perpetrators of Genocide in the Reflection of their Post-War Prosecution in West Germany. The 'Euthanasia' and 'Aktion Reinhard' Cases* (The Hague/London/Boston: Martinus Nijhoff 1996), 21.

9 See the website *Justiz- und NS-Verbrechen: Schwerpunkte der Strafverfolgung (Westdeutschland)*, www1.jur.uva.nl/junsv/StrafverfolgungBRD.htm.

10 For this group, see: Michael Wildt, *Generation des Unbedingten. Das Führungskorps des Reichssicherheits-Hauptamtes* (Hamburg: Hamburger Edition 2003), passim.

11 Bloch, M., J. Houwink ten Cate and H.G. van der Wilt, 'Iwan Demjanjuk voor de Rechtbank', in: *Nederlands Juristenblad*, 2010/44,45, 2282-2288.

12 Streit, C., *Keine Kameraden: die Wehrmacht und die sowjetischen Kriegsgefangenen 1941-1945* (Stuttgart: Deutsche Verlagsanstalt, 1978).

13 This was the case with one of the three surviving Trawniki men living in Germany, Samuel Kunz.

14 See endnote xi.

15 Langer, H., *Schlussvortrag*, Munich District Court, March 23, 2011, 6-7.

16 Landgericht München II, *Urteil der 1. Strafkammer des Landgerichts München II in der Strafsache gegen Demjanjuk, John, wegen Beihilfe zum Mord*, Munich 2011.

17 On this region, see Amir Weiner, *Making Sense of War: The Second World War and the Fate of the Bolshevik Revolution* (Princeton: Princeton University Press, 2001), passim.

18 See Houwink ten Cate, J., 'The Activities of Wachmann John Demjanjuk (1940-1952)', www.chgs.nl, 26; *Urteil*, 173.

19 For what is by far the best overview of this complicated case, see Gitta Sereny, 'The Case of John Demjanjuk', in: Sereny, *The German Trauma: Experiences and Reflections, 1938-2000* (London: Allen Lane, 2000).

20 Schelvis, J. (with Bob Moore), *Sobibor: A History of a Nazi Death Camp* (London: Berg, 2007), passim.

21 There are – as far as I know – two exceptions: a trial against three Lithuanians and the trial of the ethnic German Franz Swidersky.

22 'A Very Ordinary Henchman: Demjanjuk Trial to Break Legal Ground in Germany', in: *Der Spiegel*, 10 July 2009. See: *Landgericht Bonn*, 8 Ks 3/62, 23. Juli 1965, in: Sagel-Grande, I., H.H. Fuchs and C.F. Rüter (eds.), *Justiz und NS-Verbrechen. Sammlung deutscher Strafurteile wegen nationalsozialistischer Tötungsverbrechen 1945-1966*, Bd. xxi, Lfd. Nr. 594 [German]. The other recent German court cases against German and non-German Nazi criminals do not deal with complicity in murder, but with co-perpetratorship ('Mittäterschaft') in murder.

23 For the indictment, see www.xoxol.org/dem/munich-docs/munich-docs-index.html. See also 'Son of Nazi Victim Testifies at Demjanjuk Trial', Associated Press, 1 December 2009; 'Alleiniger Daseinszweck, Juden umzubringen' (interview with Prof.Dr. Cornelius Nestler), *Der Spiegel*, 14 February 2010 [German].

24 Black, P., 'Die Trawniki-Männer und die "Aktion Reinhard"', in: Bogdan Musial (ed.), *'Aktion Reinhard'. Der Völkermord an den Juden im Generalgouvernement 1941-1944* (Osnabrück: Fibre Verlag, 2004) [German]; David Alan Rich, 'Reinhard's Footsoldiers: Soviet Trophy Documents and Investigative Records as Sources', in: Roth, J.K. and E. Maxwell (eds.), *Remembering the Future: The Holocaust in an Age of Genocide*, vol. 1 (Houndmills, Basingstoke and New York: Palgrave, 2001). Further publications by Peter Black include: Black, 'Police Auxiliaries for Operation Reinhard: Shedding Light on the Trawniki Training Camp through Documents from Behind the Iron Curtain', in: Bankier, D. (ed.), *Secret Intelligence and the Holocaust* (New York: Enigma Books/Jerusalem: Yad Vashem, 2006), 327-366; Black, 'Askaris in the 'Wild East': The Deployment of Auxiliaries and the Implementation of Nazi Racial Policy in Lublin District', in: Ingrao, C. and F.A.J. Szabo (eds.), *The Germans and the East* (West Layette, Indiana: Purdue University Press, 2007), 277-309. Blacks most recent contribution on the Trawniki men was published in the beginning of 2011; Black, P., 'Foot Soldiers of the Final Solution: The Trawniki Training Camp and Operation Reinhard', in: *Holocaust and Genocide Studies*, 25, no. 1 (Spring 2011), 1-99. This is an extended and richly annotated version of the article Black published in 2004.

25 See www.nizkor.org/ftp.cgi/people/d/danilchenko.ignat.t. See also 'Doubt Cast on Auto Worker's Nazi Ties,' CBS News, 18 March 2010. On the credibility of Soviet legal sources, see Alexander Victor Prusin, "'Fascist Criminals to the Gallows!'': The Holocaust and Soviet War Crimes Trials, December 1945-February 1946', in: *Holocaust and Genocide Studies* 17, 1 (Spring 2003): 1-30; Tanja Penter, "Local Collaborators on Trial: Soviet War Crimes Trials under Stalin (1943-1953)," *Cahiers du Monde russe* 49, 2-3 (April-September 2008): 1-24.]

26 *Urteil*,157.

27 See note 24.

28 Grabitz, H., 'Iwan Demjanjuk zum Tode verurteilt. Anmerkungen zur strafrechtlichen Verantwortung der "Trawnikis"', *Tribüne. Zeitschrift zum Verständniss des Judentums*, 27, Heft 108 (1988), 176-182.

29 Apart from Demjanjuk these men were Samuel Kunz, a guard in Belzec (now deceased) and Karpo Nagorny, an alleged guard in Flossenbürg.

30 For estimates, see Schelvis and Moore, *Sobibor*.

31 *Urteil*,118.

32 There is one exception, Alexei Vaitzen (Weitzen) who lives in Ryazan in the Russian Federation, but the condition of his memory is unclear. Furthermore, it is surprising that Vaitzen did not come forward as a possible witness at an earlier point; 'Russian Says He Recalls Demjanjuk from Death Camp', Reuters, 12 February 2010.

33 Communication to the author by Mr. Manuel Bloch.

34 Maathuis, M., 'Advocaat tegen de duivel' (interview with mr. Manuel Bloch), in: *Nederlands Juristenblad*, October, 14, 2011, 21-23.

35 *Urteil*, 132-135.

36 *Urteil*, 140-143.

37 *Urteil*, 150-153.

38 *Urteil*, 155, 174-177.

39 *Urteil* 157.

40 *Urteil*, 158.

41 *Urteil*, 177.

42 Jules Schelvis, *Vernietigingskamp Sobibor. De Transportlijsten*, Amsterdam 2001.

43 *Urteil*, 113-117.

44 *Urteil*, 199.

45 *Urteil*, 181.

46 *Urteil*, 181.

47 *Urteil*, 191.

48 *Urteil*, 196.
49 *Urteil*, 183.
50 *Urteil*, 195.
51 See note xxxiv.

About the authors

BART VAN DER BOOM (b. 1964) is Associate Professor at the Institute for History of Leiden University. He specializes in modern Dutch political history, in particular the history of the German Occupation. He has published on the city of The Hague during the Second World War, Dutch civil defense during the Cold War and more recently on ordinary Dutchmen and the Holocaust.

PIM GRIFFIOEN (b. 1963) studied at VU University in Amsterdam and received his MA in history in 1993, after which he worked at the Ghetto Fighters' House Museum, Archives and Study Center in Israel. Since 1997 he has worked as a contract researcher for the Netherlands Institute for War Documentation (NIOD), the Netherlands Organization for Scientific Research (NWO), and the University of Konstanz. He received his PhD in History from the University of Amsterdam in 2008. He was a postdoctoral research fellow at Yad Vashem, Jerusalem, and is currently a visiting scholar at the Institute for Advanced Study Konstanz/Kulturwissenschaftliches Kolleg Konstanz.

WICHERT TEN HAVE (b. 1944) is a historian and director of Holocaust and Genocide Studies at the NIOD Institute for War, Holocaust and Genocide Studies. In 1999, he was awarded his PhD for research into the Nederlandsche Unie, a political movement that called for cooperation with the Nazis during the German occupation of the Netherlands. As a lecturer, he is also associated with the master's programme in Holocaust and Genocide Studies at the University of Amsterdam.

JOHANNES HOUWINK TEN CATE (b. 1956) studied contemporary and socio-economic history at the University of Utrecht, the Netherlands. He worked as a PhD student at the Institute for European History in Mainz. Since 1989 his primary topic of interest has been the Nazi persecution of the Jews in the occupied Dutch territories. He is currently working on a book on that topic. Since 2002 he has been Professor of Holocaust and Genocide Studies at the University of Amsterdam.

MARIEKE MEEUWENOORD (b. 1978) studied twentieth century history at the University Utrecht. Her PhD-research at the Centre for Holocaust and Genocide Studies in Amsterdam was a historical-sociological study of *Konzentrationslager Herzogenbusch*: camp Vught. During her research she held several lectures both at national and international levels, and she published several articles. She took her doctoral degree in June 2011 and is now working on the publication of her PhD-thesis called *People, power and mentalities behind barbed-wire. A historical-sociological study of camp Vught (1943-1944)*.

PETER ROMIJN (b. 1955) is Director of Research at the NIOD Institute of War, Holocaust and Genocide Studies and professor of Twentieth-Century History at the University of Amsterdam, the Netherlands. He has published on the political purges in the post-war Netherlands, on the persecution of Dutch Jews, on the political history of occupation and on late-colonial issues. With Hans Blom he was responsible for the NIOD report on the Dutch involvement in the Bosnian War and the Fall of Srebrenica (1995).

RON ZELLER (b. 1952) was educated at the Amsterdam social academy. During a career in the Dutch civil service he studied contemporary history and museum studies at VU University in Amsterdam. He worked as a contract researcher for the Netherlands Institute for War Documentation (NIOD), the Netherlands Organization for Scientific Research (NWO), and the University of Konstanz. He received his PhD in History from the University of Amsterdam in 2008. Currently he is a visiting scholar at the Institute for Advanced Study Konstanz/Kulturwissenschaftliches Kolleg Konstanz.